T0356290

THE
SECOND
SHOT

THE SECOND SHOT

A GREEN BERET'S LAST MISSION

GENE YU

Little
a

Published by Little A, New York

www.apub.com

Amazon, the Amazon logo, and Little A are trademarks of Amazon.com, Inc., or its
affiliates.

ISBN-13: 9781662510564 (hardcover)
ISBN-13: 9781662510540 (paperback)
ISBN-13: 9781662510557 (digital)

Cover design by Isaac Tobin
Cover image: © Patrick Hendry / Unsplash; © Hans Eiskonen / Unsplash;
© Krystal Ng / Unsplash

Printed in the United States of America

First edition

for the next generation

Due to my former service and its associated
security clearances, this book required government
review from the Department of Defense Office of
Prepublication and Security Review. Their redactions
are included as amended.

Contents

AUTHOR'S NOTE

Before I began this project, writers with far more experience than I had warned me about the minefields involved in writing a memoir. Our memories sometimes fail us, as do the memories of those whose stories we gather and weave into our own. Our biases, about others and about ourselves, can sometimes color our recollections.

To the degree possible, I've tried to calibrate the stories in this book. I've taken pains to test my memory against those of others who were involved directly in the events depicted. As much as possible, I have melded those views in order to create what I believe is an accurate picture of a chaotic and confusing time, even for events where I was not present.

I've certainly condensed some of the events in the book, and, occasionally, I've taken steps to disguise the identity of certain participants. Such is the nature of things when you're telling a tale that is, at least in part, about the War on Terror. With both an audit by a United States Department of Defense legal review and authorization from senior Philippine intelligence officers, I'm confident that none of the information contained in this book could expose intelligence or jeopardize any future operations.

One of my chief objectives in taking on this project was to celebrate the exploits of the Philippine Scout Rangers and the nation's National Intelligence Coordinating Agency (NICA) operatives, and to do honor to kidnapped Taiwanese tourist Chang An-Wei, known as Evelyn

Chang, and her heroic family. Still, what appears in these pages only scratches the surface. Even now I keep summoning an image of Evelyn, faced with unspeakable cruelty, isolated and threatened, kept at one point bound in a boat under a moonless sky, looking up at the heavens and finding the strength in her Buddhist faith to forgive her kidnappers. An entire book could be written about just that one moment.

Likewise, an image keeps coming back to me about how, on the day of the rescue, NICA analyst ███████████████████, a desk jockey for all intents and purposes, risked his life for a stranger, effectively allowing himself to be held hostage for several hours by hardened killers from the Abu Sayyaf terrorist group, all to save a woman he'd never heard of until just days ago. His name, like other terms throughout the text deemed classified by the US Department of Defense, has been redacted.

I have only the space of one book to tell this entire saga. But the truth is, the stories behind the stories, of triumphs and of survival that I only touch on, could fill an entire library. These are full, rich, and important stories that need to be told, need to be heard, need to be written. I hope someday they will be.

Of course, I had another objective in writing this story. We now live in a time of extreme division and racial and ethnic hostility, especially in America. Hate crimes of all stripes are up, including incidents involving the Asian community. I have lived and worked in seven countries across the Asia-Pacific region over twenty years, and the difference in how Asians are treated as a minority in the States is starkly apparent to me. One quiet yet corrosive bias depicts Asian males—and Asian American males in particular—as docile, meek, or frail, suited for intellectual pursuits, perhaps, but somehow "less than" the image of the classic American male. I believe this pervasive stereotype has invited random attacks of Asians on the streets without fear of repercussion or retaliation. I feel that the platform given to me after the Evelyn Chang case has placed on me a responsibility. I have the opportunity to confront those pernicious stereotypes head-on in this book and to help shape a different narrative.

As I grow older, I become more protective of my privacy, but I hope that sharing my journey will also help nudge other Asians to tell their vastly more inspiring stories. I know they are out there because I am proud to call many of them my friends. I certainly cannot change the narrative alone. We are a humble and self-effacing community, but it is past time to be heard and seen.

This is not an easy task. Failure is always a risk when you chart a new course, and I have tried, throughout this book, to accurately depict my own shortcomings—which were many—and to do so in a way that is both rigorously honest and, I hope, occasionally entertaining.

You can judge whether I have succeeded.

Gene Yu
2024
San Francisco, California
USA

POM POM ISLAND, MALAYSIA

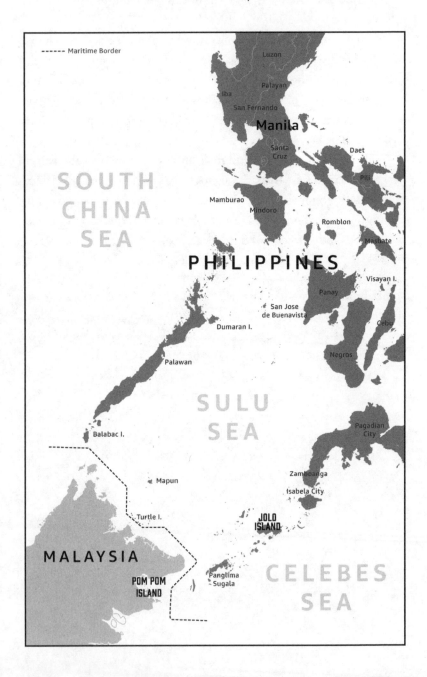

Prologue

Rescue Me

Maybe it was the gentle, rhythmic lapping of the moonlit waters of the inlet or the sumptuous meal she had just shared with Eric Hsu, her common-law husband and life partner of twenty years, surrounded by the doting and attentive waitstaff at Malaysia's Pom Pom Island Resort. For a week now, the Taiwanese couple had been feted and fussed over, treated like royalty, and for the first time in her fifty-odd years, Evelyn Chang felt like a queen rather than a virtually invisible general manager at a factory on the Chinese mainland. Curled up in Eric's arms as the waxing moon dipped into the peaceful sea, the lifelong factory girl fell into a deep sleep.

As long as Evelyn—or anyone else—could remember, she had been dreaming of this magical escape to a tropical paradise. Her whole life, it seemed, had been marked by deferring personal gratification. She had always denied herself the little luxuries that everyone else indulged in. Even with simple pleasures like food, Evelyn had been the picture of self-restraint, although her diabetes might have had something to do with that. Rarely, if ever, had she done anything just for herself. Her finances wouldn't permit it. Nor would her health.

But when she finally retired, she got herself a fresh perm and rewarded herself with a ten-day trip of a lifetime, the equivalent of US$438 a night, a hefty sum for most. Of all the island resorts scattered across the seas in that corner of the world, she had chosen this place in Malaysian Borneo because it seemed so remote and peaceful, isolated by one hundred nautical miles of ocean from the seething political turmoil and violence that marked the restive archipelago of the western Philippines.

She had not been disappointed. It was beautiful, and from the moment she and Eric landed at the airport, Evelyn had felt special. Porters had scrambled to carry their luggage. Their driver, the staff at the resort—everyone had seemed so welcoming, so guileless, almost to the point of obsequiousness. Of course, Evelyn Chang was guileless too.

It never dawned on her that hidden beneath all those forced smiles might be something else. Resentment. Malice. Greed. Evelyn was far too trusting, and far too intoxicated by the excitement of her retirement vacation, to consider that even this magical place had an underworld, an invisible network spanning hundreds of miles of open ocean between Pom Pom Island and the terrorists, cutthroats, and kidnappers located in the nearby Sulu Archipelago, a chain of islands in the southernmost part of the Philippines. Evelyn was unaware, like most tourists visiting this area of Malaysia, that one of the countless smiling faces she had encountered between the airport and the villa could—for a price—choose to betray her.

And so on the night of November 13, 2013, halfway through her ten-day sojourn in paradise, Evelyn slept soundly. She never heard the asthmatic chattering of an old skiff's motor as it raced toward her cottage, or the tiny boat slamming against the pilings that supported the rustic vacation villa, a bamboo hut on stilts projecting over the serene waters. She didn't hear the guttural orders barked by one of the young men aboard the skiff, who was so excited by the prospect of snatching a wealthy foreigner that he didn't bother to muffle his voice.

This band of underfed, undereducated, mostly teenage pirates imagined themselves as heroic jihadists, and they were indeed a faction of the terrorist organization known as Abu Sayyaf, a group able to claim it was originally endorsed by Osama bin Laden and the Southeast Asian arm of ISIS. Of course, they had long since fallen from whatever grace that might have been afforded them in the netherworld of Islamist extremists, and they were now just a renegade gang from a lawless region in the southern Philippines who had turned the kidnapping of foreigners into a cottage industry.

They operated with increasing impunity across the border in eastern Malaysian Borneo, where locals who worked at the resort, many of them fellow ethnic Tausūgs, might willingly share information about guests with Abu Sayyaf, or anyone else, for a price. Government officials had little taste for confronting the terrorists. They were wary of them. But like many other restive parts of the world grappling with national unity and territorial conflict in the wake of European colonialism, northeastern Malaysian Borneo used to be part of the Sultanate of Sulu before the British and Spanish invaders split the Tausūg nation apart between the newly formed colonies of Malaysia and the Philippines. So officials needed to consider the local sensitivities as well, especially as territorial claims are still unresolved.

As the majority-Catholic Philippines has never been able to subdue the southern Muslim region, Malaysia rightly fears both governments' lack of control of the area, and a potential repeat of a 1970s insurgent threat from the Sulu people to reunite, spilling the Philippines' forever problem over to Malaysian territory. Even as recently as February 2013 earlier that year, approximately two hundred armed Filipino individuals, identifying themselves as the Royal Security Forces of the Sultanate of Sulu, asserted historical claim on the territory and landed in Sabah, fighting with Malaysian security forces, resulting in the deaths of scores of people. Thus, the local Malaysian authorities saw no good reason to risk alienating their own Tausūg people by taking too hard a stand and kept only a small military outpost in the area, hardly sufficient to catch the speedboats of Abu Sayyaf kidnappers.

But the likely primary driver of this lack of security posture was far less political. Malaysia was heavily investing in bolstering its growing tourism industry, and like everywhere, money drives everything. Minimal security prevented frightening off tourists and their tourist dollars, especially the many scuba divers who flock to nearby Sipadan Island, one of the most famous and beautiful coral reef diving spots in the world. They'd make halfhearted attempts in the wake of significant kidnappings, sure. But those were mostly pantomimes for the press, a sputtering denunciation of the crime, followed by an eagerness to suppress the story's impact on tourism cash flow, and likely a few officials' personal bank accounts—a typical scenario where Southeast Asian politics, security, and business converge.

Across the border in the Philippines, people didn't have much more appetite for battling the terrorists, at least not then. The primary military domestic effort was against the New People's Army, the longest-running communist insurgency in the world, a much larger and organized rebel force with guerrilla camps all across the Philippine islands. The conventional wisdom was that Abu Sayyaf required less of the broader military's efforts to contain. The Abu Sayyaf fortunes had sunk even further a few weeks earlier when they lost a large-scale assault operation in a major battle and attempted occupation of the desolate southern Philippine city of Zamboanga, a decisive engagement that had seen the worst urban fighting in the country since World War II.

The members of Abu Sayyaf were still licking their wounds from that defeat, but oddly enough, the group was also attracting new recruits at an alarming rate, undoubtedly expecting that—in addition to lining its pockets—this latest kidnapping would restore some luster to a tarnished reputation. They had never distinguished themselves for their planning or their precision, but what they lacked in military discipline and dedication to their mission, they made up for in chaos and cruelty. On far too many occasions, they had lost interest in their captives, discovered that they weren't worth the time and expense of maintaining, and simply executed them. Incessant rape and sexual abuse were also considered standard operating procedure, particularly with foreign women. Beheadings—recorded on video and circulated globally—were not uncommon.

But this time, they thought they had somebody worth snatching, somebody whom someone would be willing to pay to get back.

For Evelyn, it was all a blur: the deafening report of AK-47 fire echoing against the polished teak walls, the gasps of her husband, her own screams, the harsh and vicious barking of the terrorists as they grabbed her so brutally that they broke her wrist.

Nothing in her whole life had prepared her for the moment when a gang of murderous kidnappers would storm her villa, kick open the flimsy screen door, and barge in with automatic rifles blazing. For when eight rounds tore into Eric's face and chest, killing him instantly. But in the chaos and confusion, she had either not seen him slaughtered or, in her trauma, had simply erased the memory of his murder. In any case, it would be weeks before she would understand that he was dead.

A bag was thrown over Evelyn's head. She could barely breathe as her kidnappers dragged her through the shattered and bullet-riddled door and down the slippery steps, then tossed her into their waiting boat for the short but seemingly endless trip across placid, moonlit waters and through the jungle, eventually to a remote camp in a lawless no-man's-land in the Philippines.

The terrorists menaced Evelyn for days, dragging her through trackless jungle, a one-woman Bataan Death March. Her kidnappers were buoyed by the certainty that once they made contact with her loved ones, their fortunes would be made, while Evelyn—battered and in agony from her broken wrist, in shock and terrified, too weak and confused even to cry out—stumbled through the thick undergrowth like a zombie.

At one point, an Abu Sayyaf terrorist, no older than a teenager, reached into Evelyn's shirt to molest her—she snatched his hand and instinctively shouted at him, "I am your grandma!" Shocked, the boy soldier instantly recoiled, and Evelyn escaped sexual assault throughout her entire captivity. Unwittingly, Evelyn tapped into two saving graces: First, she humanized herself to her captors. And second, she triggered the Confucian values of filial piety and respect for elders that even Abu Sayyaf kidnappers could not ignore from their culture.

Nevertheless, she was sold from one Abu Sayyaf subgroup to another, until finally she stumbled through a perimeter, past guards who hurled fresh abuse at her, and into a camp with approximately eighty Abu Sayyaf fighters.

She'd lost all sense of time. She could not have said how many days had passed since she had been taken from her vacation villa. She had no idea where she'd been, and no clue where she was.

But I did. I knew this corner of the world. I knew the kidnappers as well as I knew myself. In fact, at that low point in my life, I probably knew the kidnappers *better* than I knew myself.

My name is Gene Yu. I am the founder and CEO of Blackpanda Group, a leading cybersecurity company in Asia, with offices in Singapore, Hong Kong, Tokyo, and Manila. Our lead investors are two multibillion-dollar global private equity firms, Primavera Venture Partners and Gaw Capital Partners. We are local and specialized cybersecurity emergency responders, and through our partnership with the Lloyd's of London syndicate Chaucer, we also built the first pure cybersecurity insurance firm in the region: Pandamatics Underwriting. We have made it our mission to democratize cybersecurity resilience across

Asia by combining a services, technology, and insurance company all in one.

I am proud of Blackpanda's achievements. And I'm grateful for the minor notoriety that those achievements have brought me. But the truth is that in this part of the world, where I now live and work, I am still best known as the man who assembled a team of Philippine special forces operators, a handful of colorful and erratic soldiers of fortune, and, under the nose of officials in Taiwan, Malaysia, and the Philippines, engineered an unsanctioned mission to rescue Evelyn Chang.

It was a dramatic—at times desperate—operation that made international headlines and became, in many ways, the stuff of myth. It's been embroidered and distorted over the years; half-truths have been passed off as fact, and comforting falsehoods have taken on the patina of history. But enough years have passed that I believe it's time to peel away the myths and finally tell the whole story about what really happened in the jungles near Mindanao.

With the Evelyn Chang case, I had to come face-to-face with a lot of my own myths, stories I had told myself over the years to justify all the times I had come up short. I had to come to terms with my history, all the times I had made myself a willing hostage to my two cultures, to my family, to my community, to the image of an American military officer that had been beaten into me at West Point, and to the myths that I embraced and believed as a team leader in the Green Berets. I was held hostage by the ghosts of my exit from the military under a cloud of suspicion, and I was held hostage by the secret knowledge that even my so-called successes in the military had sown the seeds of other failures. Indeed, I had once engaged in a battle against the very same terrorists who kidnapped Evelyn Chang and been praised for it. But I had been part of a wider failure to wipe them out completely, a failure to kill their leaders. And now here I was, facing them and their followers again.

But even that will be only part of the story. The myth we're going to tackle in these pages is the media accounts of the rescue and the events that followed: Gene Yu, the action figurine, the hero, the cagey special forces operator, some kind of Asian Jason Bourne. I'd be lying if I said I'm not flattered by the image that's been crafted around me in the years since Evelyn Chang's rescue. But I'd also be lying if I pretended that it was all true.

The real truth is far more interesting. At the precise moment I was dragged into the kidnapping, I was at rock bottom in my life, failing in my transition back to the real world from my military life: adrift, lost, nearly broke, and couch surfing. For the first half of my life, I had been the typical Asian American kid, born to immigrant Taiwanese parents in Boston, raised in Concord, and then transported to the gilded Asian American suburbs around Silicon Valley. I was programmed to be compliant, obedient, and successful, and I tried my best to do what was expected of me. I played tennis, because it was safe, and I mastered computers by the time I was a teenager, because that's what Asian kids do in America. But there was another part of me that rebelled against the strictures placed on me by my family, my community, and my culture. That part of me was unalloyed American, independent, at times sullen and moody, rebellious and insolent, acting as if I were certain of every decision, even—perhaps especially—when I was riddled with self-doubt. For most of my life, the Asian Gene Yu and the American Gene Yu were in open conflict, one sabotaging the other, both unsure which one to be. They may have remained locked in combat forever if I had not been accidentally but inevitably drawn into Evelyn Chang's kidnapping, against my own best instincts and in defiance of the edict of my Confucian mother, who still on occasion issues orders as though I were a child, a phenomenon I suspect all Asians have experienced. Even then, had I not learned to let go, to lead by allowing others to lead, the story may have ended very differently.

The myth that's grown up around me in the years since the operation in the Philippines is the myth of the man who rescued Evelyn Chang. But the truth is that she was not the only one rescued when a courageous team of soldiers breached the perimeter of that terrorist encampment. So was I. And this is the story of both rescues.

CONCORD, MA

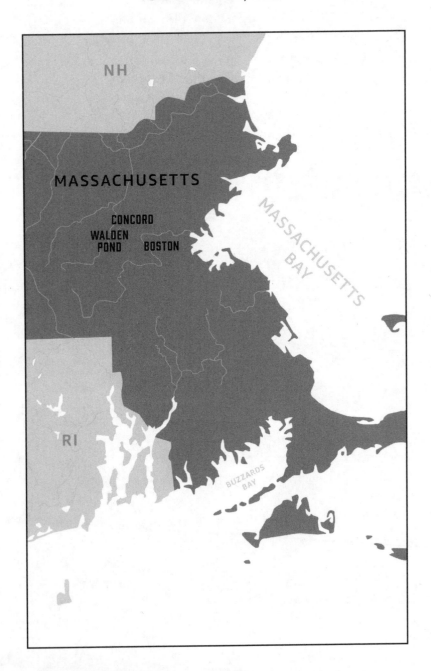

Chapter 1

Born a Foreigner

I have this image of myself as a boy. It's not so much a memory as a picture in my mind's eye, like an old Polaroid that you find at the bottom of a drawer or slipped inside the jacket of a book you can't remember reading. Like so many old pictures, it's charming in a way, though ridiculous without context.

It's a frigid New England morning. I'm seven, maybe eight, standing at attention at the foot of a neighbor's front-yard flagpole, Old Glory whipping in the icy Massachusetts wind. I'm saluting, or at least what I took then to be a salute, before West Point taught me that Americans—who have never surrendered their arms on the battlefield—show nothing but the backs of our hands. I see myself as I was then, a little yellow tin soldier shivering in the cold as he tries to be the perfect American boy.

When I think of my own story, this is where it begins, as far from Asia as you can get, in both distance and culture, without leaving the planet. Concord is a sleepy little colonial town, an hour or so west of Boston on Route 2, where the first shots of the Revolutionary War were fired. This Currier and Ives woodcut of the American dream was a crucible for me. It's the place where I was born. And in a way, I was born a foreigner, steeped—like every child born at Emerson Hospital—with that flinty sense of self-reliance, patriotism, and pride that infuses everything in Concord.

And yet I was different: an Asian kid in America's cradle. I wanted to be fully a part of that place. Indeed, it was that desperate craving to be a full American, in America's birthplace, that forced me some mornings, the way I remember it, to stop at the base of that flagpole before I trudged the thirty minutes to school across the frozen Massachusetts tundra—in my memory it's always winter—snap to attention, salute, and, in a sniffling, reedy little-boy's voice, intone the Pledge of Allegiance.

As a child, I was always treated as a foreigner by my community, both externally and internally. Teachers would ask me "How do you do it in your country?" Friends and tormentors presumed I knew something about life in China. Even my family instilled the message that we were Chinese, criticizing me when I did not inherently know a Chinese custom, derisively referring to me as "American."

As I think back on it now, I don't know for sure whether I performed this ritual for my own benefit—to reassure myself that I was, in fact, an American kid—or to convince anyone who might have been spying on me that I really was one of them, despite my appearance and my background.

It must have been an odd sight, this scrawny little Asian kid with a perpetually runny nose, in the heart of New England, doing a full Norman Rockwell—pledge and all—at the foot of the flagpole on Black Duck Road. Of course, the sight of any Asian in Concord was somewhat unusual then, which would be driven home each day after I pulled off my mittens and peeled off the sweaters and coats and scarves my mother had swaddled me in, hanging them carefully in my classroom and joining my predominantly white classmates to recite the pledge for the second time each day.

There were, as I recall, just two of us Asian kids in my class: me and a half-Japanese kid named Koji Bamba, who was trying just as hard as I was to be an American. Our first-grade teacher made sure we sat together, in the corner. In her defense, I suspect she thought we'd feel more comfortable as a team, and indeed, we did forge an alliance. And although our lives have taken us down very different paths in the decades since Concord, we've pretty much been friends since we first met, when he made me the most Asian gift ever: an origami crane. I don't recall any hostility in the classroom, no racial animus. If anything, Koji and I were granted a very limited kind of status, as if we were exotic.

My teachers, for example, seemed to have bought into the myth that all Asian kids are naturally smart. As is typical with kids from Asian households, I studied much harder than my majority-white classmates and believed I must be a prodigy by comparison. Never mind the first time I brought back a B from Alcott Elementary School on a report card, and my mother put me on my knees with my face forced to be inches from the living room corner for hours until my father returned home to give me a proper scolding and spanking—while my white friends were outside playing kickball in the street, wondering where I was. I thought I was born a genius, rather than simply outworking my classmates, and my teachers graded me accordingly.

I don't think I even experienced the kind of normal conflict—petty bullying, that sort of thing—that marks most American childhoods, and certainly not the typical bullying that occurs for many Asian kids. It was because I instinctively leaned into an image that I abhor today. One time some much older kids at Alcott Elementary School approached Koji and me—both runts, as it were—menacing us and preparing to bully us with the usual unimaginative "go back to China," cracking their knuckles, and loosening up their punching arms. Out of panic, we began vigorously mimicking martial arts moves and sounds, a pre-pubescent mash-up of bits we had seen in *The Karate Kid*, old Jackie

Chan movies, and Bruce Lee highlight reels, our only images of Asian men. America taught me as a child that the only way an Asian male could possibly be strong enough to be respected was to have a mysterious, unexplainable power nobody else knew about, which was kung fu or karate. Without this magic trick, we were not strong enough to lead. Even today, nearly forty years later, I still do not observe any global images of a strong Asian male character without the subtle additive of a flying kick or secret ninja move that acts like an invisible and apologetic crutch to our masculinity.

The older, bigger boys literally ran away. I suspect they simply assumed that because we were yellow guys, our ninja chops were not to be questioned. No one really messed with us after that, and I continued to exploit the misconception that my white classmates held that all Asians were genetically wired to be lethal in hand-to-hand combat. It was nonsense, of course. And I certainly knew it. Only recently did I realize that my fear of being found out drove me to a lifetime of studying Brazilian jiujitsu—since 1996—so I've still somehow been vectored into this archetype in the end anyway.

Even then, I felt a kind of tension, as if no matter how American I tried to be, no matter how American I truly was, I would always have a sense that I was just a little bit outside the more common American experience. I didn't really mind it back then. I loved living in New England in the 1980s, and when I pledged allegiance twice a day, I was pledging it to the nation that had given us Larry Bird and the Celtics, to the idea of America, an idea that had drawn my parents here from Taiwan for graduate school and let us build a new life on the other side of the world.

In America I was shielded from the chaos of the world my grandparents had left behind. It wouldn't be until years later that I learned how far our family had come, fleeing the war in China, finding sanctuary and gaining status in Taiwan. Three short generations later, I was speaking English and spending idyllic Sundays at Walden Pond, dreaming about building a log cabin in the woods like Thoreau, to live out my days in quiet contemplation as fiery autumn leaves fell to the ground around me. What I didn't realize then was that places like Concord, timeless places that seem to reflect an ancient glory trapped in amber, are the exception in America. I was pledging allegiance to a restless place, a nation that not only permitted us—me—to reinvent ourselves but almost demanded that we do so.

And soon enough we did. I was still a child when my father heard the siren call of Silicon Valley. His career led us to Cupertino, the birthplace of Apple, one of the largest companies in the world today. Suddenly, that comforting cauldron of clam-chowder patriotism that I had been nurtured in turned upside down and spilled out into the California sunlight. I immediately discovered that Hollywood had misled me again. Instead of the endless sea of blond, blue-eyed surfer boys that I had been led to expect by *The Karate Kid*, I was surprised to show up to my first day at school and see rows and rows of kids who looked like me: black hair, brown eyes, slightly tanner than the white kids. Everybody took school extremely seriously, particularly math and science, a radical departure from the more literary, liberal arts bent of my schooling in the Northeast.

In my mind's eye, I have another picture of myself, this time as a sullen teen out of place in a place where I should, by all appearances, have been right at home. The kid in this picture wears a ridiculous long black coat. I am pimply faced, with long, greasy hair that I let go wild in an act of good old-fashioned American teen defiance, I suppose, against my father. I remember the night he ordered me to cut it and threatened me with the back of his hand—corporal punishment remains a treasured tool of child-rearing in Confucian households—and I remember spitting curses at him under my breath: "Fuck you! I'm *never* cutting it." Of course, I took care to make sure he couldn't really hear me, for fear of what might happen if he did. I stormed out, my hair intact, my peculiarly American adolescent angst on full display. I had become a full-fledged American teen, James Dean facing off against Jim Backus in *Rebel Without a Cause*.

I thought I had won that round. But not really.

All I had won was the right to paint myself as even more of an outsider. The truth is, I felt no less a foreigner than I had as a young child in Concord. Awkward, sullen, desperate to win the attention of the pretty girls in my class, I didn't realize that my clothes and my hair and my attitude all but guaranteed that they wouldn't give me a second look, except perhaps to snicker at my appearance.

My early life in Concord had left me ill prepared to spend my teen years in one of the most intense Asian American bubbles in the States, the southern region of the Bay Area referred to as South Bay. In Concord, I had been unique. In Cupertino, the whole culture, the community, and my family all seemed to be locked in a conspiracy to make sure that by the time I grew up, I would not be. Even the Army could have learned a thing or two about discipline from my hypercompetitive community in the concrete Asian jungle of Cupertino, an intensely driven culture of work ethic and ambition to succeed at all costs.

Cupertino had organically developed its own kind of hazing ritual. But I resisted. In response, I became many things, a slouching, sneering mass of contradictions: a greasy-haired weirdo in a trench coat who also donned tennis shorts after school and excelled on the court; a mediocre student in a sea of congenital overachievers, who somehow wormed his way into all the honors and AP classes my school offered, barely making it through. I could not keep up with Cupertino's army of academic powerhouses—everybody worked hard, much harder—and I quickly lost the sense of value I'd enjoyed in a small Massachusetts town like Concord.

In short, I was struggling, like most teenagers.

Computers offered me some sanctuary. I took programming classes at the local community college in the summers and plugged into all the computer courses offered at my high school on the ubiquitous free computers that Steve Jobs had gifted to the community. Cupertino had plenty of other Asian kids who crushed me behind the keyboard, but I participated. These were groundbreaking opportunities in the late eighties, and I suppose I took some solace in the fact that if I couldn't crack the code of the real world, I could write a new one in a virtual world.

Tennis was an escape for me, too, though not one I embraced wholeheartedly. At first, I took it as a defeat when my mother, with her native Asian mistrust of all but the most refined and respectable athletic pursuits, drove me to take up the sport. My parents had been very supportive of my athletic endeavors back in Concord; my mother had encouraged my dabbling in all the typical pursuits of American teens. Like any good New England kid, I had strapped on skis for the first time when I was about four and acquitted myself decently on the slopes, all things considered. And of course, I don't believe you're even allowed to live within driving distance of Boston without playing ice hockey. I played damned well, if I do say so myself, at least well enough to win a spot on our local all-star team as the starting center. Then there was Little League. I'll never forget swinging for the chain-link fence and nailing a grand slam in the bottom of the last inning to win a championship game. My parents still keep a picture of the moment right before I whacked it out of the park, my one and only home run in life. In that picture, I'm wielding a bright-orange foam-covered bat that looks for all the world like a pool noodle, but it remains one of my parents' cherished possessions and one of the pictures I conjure when I think of my past.

By the time I was in middle school, though, my mother's Asian instincts had begun to kick in, and slowly she tightened the reins. I was permitted two sports: soccer, which in middle school is still comparatively safe, and tennis, which, of course, is even safer.

I turned out to be a better-than-average tennis player. It wasn't that I liked the game, not particularly, but I did like the coach my mother hired for me. His name was Francisco, and he was a hard-nosed immigrant from Mexico. To this day, when I think about why I am who I am, Francisco remains one of the people whose guidance and mentorship I treasure most. And it wasn't because of what he taught me about tennis.

Francisco was one hell of a life coach. With his toughness, his commitment, and above all his loyalty, he became a friend. More than a friend. He became a big brother, at a time when I desperately needed one. My parents trusted him, too, so much so they would sometimes allow me to stay over at his place before matches or important practices. In hindsight, however, I think they recognized that this thirty-five-year-old Mexican had a natural ability to bridge the chasm between their generation and mine, a widening gap that they realized was becoming increasingly difficult to close.

To the degree that I became a good tennis player—and I did, good enough that it was one of the things that got me into West Point later as an NCAA Division I recruited athlete—it was not because of what Francisco taught me about the game. It was because he taught me *how to play the game*. He was my mentor, and I began to emulate his machismo on the court, trying to stand up to others that would dare to overlook me across the net. While the tennis courts at De Anza College were perhaps softer than the American gridiron where many of my future West Point contemporaries sharpened iron on iron as adolescents, Francisco was my first teacher who taught me how to fight for the win, whatever it took. We were a formidable team.

He introduced me to a world beyond the pampered, affluent Asian bubble that I inhabited in Cupertino. Speaking broken English—and a poetically charged, rapid-fire, caustically funny Spanish when he got excited or frustrated—Francisco would periodically drag me off to an East San Jose barrio after practice or a match. We'd sit down together for a meal at one of those places that Mexicans share only with each other, the real legit stuff that Abuela used to make. And he would talk. And I would talk. And he would listen.

I know it sounds like bragging, but I really am a very good tennis player. On the surface, it might look like I could have become even better if I'd had a coach other than Francisco at that early stage of my development. But I wouldn't have been a mentally tougher person, and I could never have found a better teacher for this. I still often imagine that I'm back in the barrio with Francisco, listening carefully to his advice. As a former amateur boxer, Francisco taught me how to be tough and how to be a winner at all costs, and the influence of his fighter's mindset led me to the ring years later.

When I slithered into high school, my mother tightened the reins even more. It was time, she said, for me to focus on academics, and that meant I could do only one sport. I had to choose between soccer and tennis. Maybe I'm remembering it incorrectly, but I don't think so. I distinctly remember my mother pushing me toward tennis, and I cried my eyes out because I loved soccer so much. I'm sure she saw tennis as the less hazardous, more civilized sport, and I suppose it is.

It always amuses me when I talk with international friends about my childhood tennis experiences in the States, because they view it as this sophisticated, global game where the players are highly respected as the world's most famous individual sport athletes. I certainly view it this way as well today and deeply appreciate the elegance and depth of the game. My ability to play well serves me on multiple fronts with both my business and social networks. And its unique lessons in self-reliance and independence undoubtedly trained me to be comfortable handling challenges as an individual operator and, later on, as an entrepreneur.

But tennis is not the sort of sport that grants one much status in American high schools, where athletics and other extracurriculars oftentimes form the basis of class structure and identity, with the most violent and dangerous sports residing at the top of the food chain. You seldom see anybody paying attention to the tennis team—it hardly qualifies as a sport in most people's eyes—and this sort of derisive treatment persisted even at West Point among the cadets. In this regard, tennis is kind of like the chess club but possibly worse off in the social hierarchy as it pathetically attempts to position itself as a sport in the American consciousness.

So when I reflect back on high school, I had something of an identity: a tennis player, yes, but an angry, sullen one with greasy hair and a trench coat. There were two fully functional and largely independent societies in my high school, and the student body was more or less equally divided between them. There were the white students, and there were the Asian kids. Despite my eccentricities, I tended to hang out among the "cool" Asian water polo and swimming jocks, who, with their more impressive sport identities, navigated Cupertino much more smoothly than I did.

No one, on either side of the gulf, thought much of tennis, despite the fact that our predominantly Asian tennis team was, by my junior year, literally the reigning champion of the entire West Coast, with our top players, including myself, ranked among the very best in the entire United States. And yet this afforded me no standing at all in the circles I traveled in. It was nice that we were champions. *Nice.* No word more quickly and cleanly emasculates a young man than the word "nice," uttered by a pretty classmate. Even with other Asians, we were just the nerdy Asian tennis team.

By my junior year, I was still impatiently waiting for a growth spurt, and though it would eventually happen, I was still a freakishly short, awkward, long-haired nobody who was often mistaken for a girl from behind. I wanted for nothing—nothing material, that is. I lived in a lovely home with a strong and, in their own traditionally Chinese way, supportive family. I could draw on not one but two rich cultures, Chinese and American, each of them appealing to the better angels of my nature. And yet I fully accepted neither. Instead, in my heart I felt as if I had no culture, no identity, and I began to let myself sink into a swamp of isolation and angst-ridden teen despair. I floated along in life, confused and frustrated all the time by my station in life.

I've learned since that businessmen are motivated by money and politicians are motivated by power. Warriors are not motivated by either. Warriors are motivated by honor. Francisco awakened the fire in my belly on those endless sprints up Rancho San Antonio's mountain trails and the hours toiling shot after shot on the concrete courts in the scorching California sun. But there was no one to confirm my honor for me—or, more accurately, I had not yet had the chance to do anything that could confirm it for myself.

But I would soon learn that identity is not something you take off a rack and wear like a trench coat. It has to be discovered. And sometimes you have to travel a very long way to find out what's really inside you.

ECUADOR

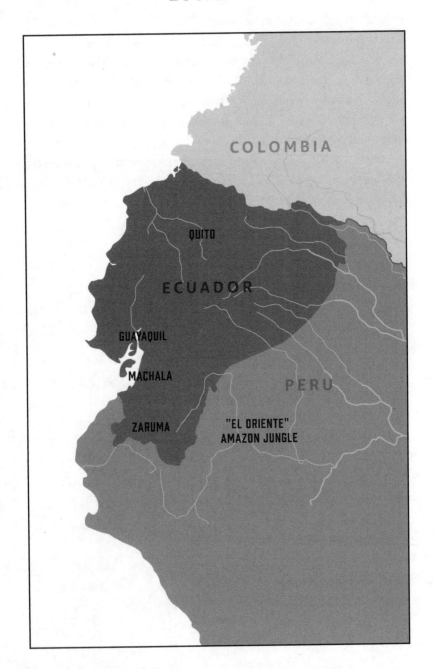

Chapter 2

The Grapefruit Express

I was searching for anything that would help me break out of my depression and ennui when one day in Spanish class, a not-for-profit organization called Amigos de las Américas showed up to give a short presentation about a summer program that sent American high school students to a rural part of Latin America to help with environmental and health projects.

It was a full-immersion program that took American kids, with their rudimentary high school Spanish, plunked them down in the middle of some remote Latin American village, and effectively said, "Adios." Most kids came from wealthy families that could afford the $4,000 price tag for the summer, but to gain entry, you had to raise the money for your own airfare and your keep as part of the spirit of organically inspired volunteer work. To do that, you had to go door-to-door in your neighborhood, selling a commodity.

Grapefruit.

I will always marvel at the thought process that had led executives from an international nonprofit to conclude that the one thing the people of South Bay needed, above all else, was easy and convenient access to a citrus fruit that literally no one in the world likes. I have never heard of anyone saying, "You know what I really want right now?

I want bitter, softball-size produce delivered to my door by a greasy-haired teenager in a trench coat."

Needless to say, I resented the hell out of the whole grapefruit hustle, and the young cynic in me suspected that among their "amigos," the nonprofit counted at least one influential Florida grapefruit company that profited handsomely from the deal. But under the surface of that cynical, teenage Gene Yu, something about the whole idea of going off to a less fortunate place and being of service appealed to me. My family was historically prosperous, the descendants of aristocratic landowners in China who had fled to Taiwan after the revolution when the communists seized everything. Although they had experienced hard times in Taiwan rebuilding from the ground up, decades before my birth, here they had found success and security, first in Boston and later in the Bay Area. And they had always maintained a commitment to the idea of service, especially the idea of serving the poor.

I don't know if that sense of obligation is imprinted in my genes, or if I picked it up simply by watching my parents, but as I watched videos of impoverished children in these remote Latin American villages, I felt a desire—the first really strong desire I had felt since moving to Cupertino—to throw myself wholly into helping people.

Of course, the simplest answer would be that Francisco's influence and stories of his poor upbringing in Mexico had led me to the desire to lend a helping hand to Latinos. But the underlying driver is simply that I love to serve and help others less fortunate than me, ideally in my own way and with my own unique skills, knowledge, and abilities, and this opportunity first awakened me to this calling inside. Indeed, the motto of the Green Berets is *De Oppresso Liber*, which means "to free the oppressed" in Latin, and these early motivations have persisted throughout my life even in my career today at Blackpanda.

As I said before, despite my lowly status as a high school tennis geek, I did have a few friends, and they thought my sudden obsession with the good works of Amigos de las Américas was, in a word, loco. Cupertino told me that good Asian boys are supposed to spend every waking hour of the summer prepping for the SATs, not galivanting off to South America to be an unpaid do-gooder, bringing uncontaminated drinking water to utter strangers. Their disapproval only motivated me more, and I spent an inordinate amount of time over the next few months hustling grapefruit like they were loose joints.

I spent my spare time dozing through interminable meetings that Amigos de las Américas intended to prepare us for the task that lay ahead. To be honest, I cannot recall a single word of those endless meetings. When I think back on it, I conjure a constant irritating drone, like the sound inside an airplane cabin, and I can still feel the mind-numbing boredom humming in my bones. The rooms were gray. The words were gray. I sometimes wonder whether it was a form of inoculation, whether the functionaries who'd designed these sessions had intended to give any young person considering a career in global social services a real taste of the bland bureaucracies that would later consume them. I will admit that the meetings prepared me for the kind I would later suffer through in the military. It surprises me even now that these sessions did nothing to dampen my enthusiasm for the adventure I was about to begin. I still remember my excitement at the beginning of that summer. While everybody else I knew was Kumon-ing themselves into a coma, I boarded a plane for a life-changing eight-week experience in rural southeastern Ecuador.

There's culture shock, and then there's the cultural tsunami I experienced, leaving the comfortable, thoroughly modern world I had come to know. Cupertino was a carefully constructed, state-of-the-art environment peopled by the best minds in Silicon Valley. The town of Zaruma consisted of a few thousand people in the summer of 1996, spooned into a crevice between mountains remote enough that it was a viable option to get there by donkey.

Here's another picture from my past. It's dawn, and I've roused myself from sleep in the little rooftop shanty that would be my home for the summer, looking out what passed for a window as a primordial fog clung to the endless rolling hills that dipped into El Oriente, the cradle of the Amazon jungle. I've been in a lot of places all over the world since that summer when I was fifteen. I've seen amazing sights in incredibly exotic places, but few have moved me as much as that first glimpse of the brooding, ancient jungle.

This is not to say that I immediately connected with the place, or that I felt anything even remotely resembling comfort. It was, you must understand, my first trip abroad, not counting a quick trip to an all-inclusive Acapulco beach resort with my parents when my younger sister and I were little, or the one time when my parents whisked me off, as a child, to Taiwan to be introduced to my relatives. In that case, I had been surrounded by family, and I was far too young to be unsettled by the experience. This was my first *real* trip abroad, and it was to a place with little running water and sporadic electricity, three hours by donkey and car from the nearest city of Machala, a place where no one had ever seen anyone who looked like me.

My host father was strict and stoic, and by the standards of Zaruma, he was erudite and worldly. He was the principal of the local high school, but he was taciturn to the point of being gruff. Six people lived in that house, including his eldest son, who sold hallucinogens on the side, and most of them were as silent as the patriarch. I don't believe he said six words to me in the eight weeks I was there. Even if he had, he could have done little to help me grasp my new surroundings, and he could do nothing to help those in Zaruma adjust to me.

It would have been hard enough if I had just been a soft American kid beamed down into this mountain village at the hard edge of the jungle, but I was also an Asian American kid, and that made me doubly foreign to the locals. I can't begin to express the real terror that I felt the first time I walked out onto the dusty street, where a group of adult men shouted the word "Chino!" and began to chase me.

It took me a while to realize that there wasn't any malice in it. It wasn't bigotry, at least not the dangerous sort. They had never seen an Asian kid before. I was like a character from a storybook, and their surprise and excitement just overcame them. But try telling that to a scrawny Taiwanese tenth grader from Cupertino who has just read *To*

Kill a Mockingbird. I was certain that I was surrounded by Asian haters who would stomp me into a paste as soon as I let my guard down. Finding a way to prove my value and move past this first real experience of being singled out for simply being Asian, and the associated stereotypes, provided the confidence to navigate around similar obstacles throughout the rest of my life.

It took a couple of weeks before I felt confident and safe enough to venture alone out of my rooftop pigeon coop, and even then, at first, it was only to go to the local high school, where I would—as I had been instructed—teach the kids about the food pyramid and drill them in critical skills like how to brush your teeth in a gentle, circular motion.

I tried to take solace in the idea that I was saving the world, one incisor at a time.

And then one day, while killing time, I spotted a few guys I had seen before. They were shooting hoops outside the house where I was staying. Back in Cupertino, I had never been much of a basketball player. I'd played more than a few pickup games and cultivated a move or two, like most Asian American boys in South Bay—and in weekend games at Kennedy Junior High School, I actually played a few times with a very young Jeremy Lin, who could hold his own against us despite being more than ten years younger—but I was certainly nothing to write home about. Fortunately for me, Ecuadorans aren't world famous at basketball, either, so when I cadged my way into a pickup game at the town basketball court, I seemed, by comparison, to be a reasonably skilled player. They had nothing to compare me to except themselves, and they were quite average.

They were so impressed with my modest skills that they insisted I immediately visit their high school coach and try out for their basketball team. Now, I mentioned that, as a rule, Ecuadorans don't play much basketball. Here's a measure of how little they play. That handful of guys I had been able to relatively hold my own against on the court were, actually, among the best players in the nation, the defending national champions, Ecuador's most fearsome ballers. They were still much better players than I was, but it was passable for me to play with them. I'm not sure what I was thinking when I tried out, and I'm not sure what they were thinking when they put me on the team. I've concluded today they were primarily being generous and inclusive hosts. I didn't get much playing time, but it didn't matter. Even warming the bench suddenly gave me status in Zaruma.

Back home, I was one of America's top junior tennis players, and nobody gave me a second look. As a nonplaying basketball player on the best team in a village in the middle of Latin America, I was suddenly a local hero. I soon discovered that it is much more enjoyable to be a large fish in a small pond than a tiny fish in the immense ocean. I also learned the value of choosing to join strong institutions that had a clearly defined identity and brand, which would reorient others from making assumptions about me simply for being Asian. I also observed that the people of Zaruma, including myself for a brief time, were much happier than any community I've ever been a part of since. Maybe there is something to the old adage that life is better, much better, if you keep it simple.

On the same streets where I had been chased a few weeks earlier, grown men now approached me respectfully and invited me into their homes for lunch. Instead of cries of "Chino," they now referred to me as "El Chinito," a title of honor. Maybe it's my imagination, but I seem to remember one or two of their pretty young daughters casting me those same smiles that I had longed for back home.

When the summer ended, I left Zaruma with a few souvenirs that I would carry for the rest of my life. One, of course, was a newfound basic fluency in Spanish. At the time, much to my family's consternation, I could barely speak any Chinese, though I had been exposed to it all my life. The other souvenir was a vague sense that I had found something unexpected in myself. It wasn't until years later that what I felt upon my departure came into focus.

Distilled to its essence, it's this: I had gone to Ecuador with the idea of doing some small service for the people who lived there, but in ways that seemed improbable even at the time, they had done an even greater service for me. And that's an experience I've had again and again in the years since. It's a principle, really, one that would be driven into me as a young officer in the military, the true essence of what it means to be a Green Beret: find yourself among a foreign people in a strange land, adapt to their ways without abandoning your own, and in the process find more of yourself than you ever imagined.

It's a lesson that would be hammered home again during the excruciating ordeal of Evelyn Chang's kidnapping. The question, of course, was whether I could sustain this new sense of self, this confidence, this sense of being somebody, when I returned home, to a place where all my life, I had been nobody squared.

BAY AREA

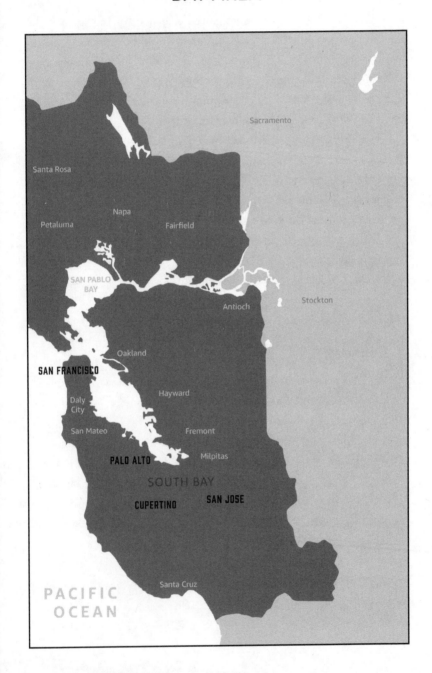

Chapter 3

Stolen Honor . . . and Duty

As I stepped off the plane in California, all I really felt was a sense that I was somehow better than I had been before I left, and a deep hunger to experience again what I had in Zaruma.

You'd think that after a two-month tour of duty in a staggeringly foreign place, coming home—to the degree that Cupertino was ever home—would have been a relief. And I won't lie to you. I often yearned for my own bed in that pigeon coop in Zaruma. I missed the old familiar faces back home, and every now and then, I'd get a sharp pang, craving some food that I recognized. There were a few moments in Ecuador when I would have given my left nut for an In-N-Out cheeseburger.

But I never felt more foreign in my own neighborhood than during those first days after I returned. Even before I ever set foot on the ground in California, I already felt a sense of loss, and maybe a bit of dread, welling up inside me. When the plane that carried me home—there's that word again—finally landed, I just sat in my seat as the other passengers disembarked. I knew that nothing I could ever do or be in Cupertino would match what I had just done. In the days that followed, I'd listen to my schoolmates drone on about their summer vacations, or catch them looking at me with a mixture of sorrow and contempt.

"Oh man, you haven't heard the new Bone Thugs-N-Harmony song? Seriously? 'Bone, bone, bone' . . . no? Where have you been?"

Where had I been? Hell, I'd just been someplace where I was *somebody*. I had started out frightened and isolated, and I had overcome fear. By the time I left, I was truly valued in Zaruma. I was unique, interesting, respected. I had finally experienced that long-awaited growth spurt, my first of two, and I now stood a full five foot nine, tanned and well toned after all that work outdoors. But the real growth spurt that summer was internal—my sense of my own worth had grown significantly. I was a basketball player and respected member of a national champion team. I was an organizer, specifically of a village-wide recycling program operating in all seven of Zaruma's schools, not that the poor people of Zaruma had a hell of a lot to recycle. When I walked through its streets—the same streets I had been chased down just weeks before—people didn't derisively call out my race; they called me *the* little Chinese guy, an honorific, a distinction I had earned. They leaned out of their windows to greet me, to invite me into their homes for an impromptu visit.

I was abruptly a nobody again with mediocre grades and a tennis racket. In Ecuador, my horizons had expanded. Back in Cupertino, they closed in on me again, and this time there was a sense of urgency for change, because I now had a sense of just how narrow my world in California was. I knew I had left something behind and that there was something better out there. If I stayed in California, I would get what every other Asian kid got out of life in Cupertino, but if I went another way, perhaps I could find something different. Something better. I knew I needed to move myself outside my comfort zone to truly grow, like I did in Ecuador, but did not know what to do or which direction I should go.

It was right around this time that I started to shoplift. Honestly, I don't really know why I did it. Maybe it was an act of silent rebellion, the sort of thing that would bring shame to my parents if I were ever caught. Maybe something in me wanted to punish them, not for anything they had done, but for all the things that I hadn't. Or maybe I just liked the thrill of it. I wasn't profligate. I didn't do it always or everywhere. I didn't pinch candy bars from the checkout line at 7-Eleven. I didn't steal CDs from the music shop or the computer store. In fact, the only place I ever regularly shoplifted was a local bookstore. A little place at The Oaks strip mall called A Clean Well-Lighted Place for Books, about a five-minute bike ride from my home next to Memorial Park. The homely shop was run by a pair of old hippies from San Francisco, glassy eyed and reeking of weed.

Somehow, I had convinced myself that stealing books was different from stealing other commodities, that because they were from the heart, books were supposed to be free, and that it was only because our society had been so corrupted by corporate culture that books had a price at all. Maybe those eight weeks spent laboring in the socialist vineyards of Ecuador had colored my perspective, or maybe I was just an entitled punk from an affluent California suburb, but in either case, I felt I had a right to slip whatever book I wanted into the copious pockets of my trench coat, and I was pretty sure that Cheech and Chong behind the counter saw things the same way I did.

And then one day, flipping through the remainder rack while the two hippies were in the back room, I committed the misdemeanor that would change my life. I came across a dog-eared copy of a book called *Honor and Duty*, written by some guy named Gus Lee. I'm not sure what drew me to it. Maybe it was the picture of the author on the back page. I had never heard of Gus Lee, an Asian guy like me but with a look in his eyes that seemed to carry both authority and serenity. He was writing about West Point, a place that had never been on my radar, not often mentioned living in the liberal enclaves of Northern California. *Honor and Duty* was novel set in the 1960s, a semifictional story about a kid who was in so many ways exactly like me, a soft Asian pretender who tore himself down and rebuilt himself into the man he wanted to be. Thumbing through the book, I suddenly felt like I had found a kindred spirit. I walked out confidently with the book in full view—in tradecraft, I'd later discover, we call this "hiding in the open"—and rushed home, where I devoured it in one sitting. And then I read it again. And again.

I had no connection at all to the US military. At the time, Monta Vista High School's principal was so antimilitary that recruiters were not even allowed on campus. I had no idea there was such a place as West Point.

As I read Lee's vivid descriptions of granite buildings in which granite leaders were built, I had a hard time believing that this school could exist. I assumed it was a figment of Lee's prodigious imagination, that he had simply conjured it, creating a kind of Hogwarts for warriors rather than wizards. When I found out that there was indeed such a place, a place where a kid like me could be all he could be, I became obsessed. I found in myself, again, the kind of drive and focus that had eluded me ever since leaving Ecuador. I had a purpose, a task, a mission in life: to become a West Pointer and to adopt an identity that I could be proud of, finally.

After odd physical fitness exams—like getting down on your knees and throwing a basketball as far as you can (seriously)—the West Point candidate may apply through a highly selective college application process, after securing a US congressional nomination. Candidates must also be perfect medical specimens and pass a comprehensive medical exam, although physical prowess can sometimes gain waivers for disqualifications—for example, a candidate can bypass asthma as a medical issue if they outperform on pull-ups or their run time. Out of the ten allowable US congressional–nominated candidates per politician, West Point admissions typically only accepts the top nominee in a second, even more stringent review process. The academy sets its bar very high, as all cadets are on a full-ride scholarship worth several hundred thousand taxpayer dollars. Demonstrated leadership potential is paramount—all but demanding that applicants have been the captain of multiple varsity teams, student body president, or, at the very least, editor in chief of the high school newspaper or yearbook. I had excelled at tennis—barely a sport in the American consciousness—so I snuck by this requirement. And by pure happenstance, my high school tennis coach was the English teacher behind the school newspaper, so I was able to secure the titles of captain of the tennis team *and* editor in chief of the newspaper. I am not sure I did any real leading in either case, but the titles looked good on my application.

I recently caught up with a West Point buddy who served as an admissions officer, and I learned more than I ever knew before about the application process. After the academy was included for the first time in 2009's *Forbes* magazine's university rankings, overall ranking number one and reminding the country of its existence, applications more than doubled, increasing competitiveness. A little-known trivia fact is that West Point, and somehow that other academy at Annapolis, used to be part of the Ivy League back in the 1930s, which was the name of the athletic conference in which they all competed. Both West Point and Annapolis voluntarily left the Ivy League after World War II as they sought out tougher sports competition than what the other nerdy schools could offer, a long-gone era where a US military officer was one of the highest-paid professions and the football teams were the best in the country. Ironically, Ivy League schools are better at most of the NCAA Division I athletics than both West Point and Annapolis today.

Nevertheless, the general median SAT score is 720 in each subject, and a significant portion of all matriculating West Point cadets are second-, third-, or even fourth-time applicants after being rejected—there are even new cadets who already have bachelor's degrees and are willing to repeat their educations for the chance to attend. Like the grading system at West Point, which is a combination of academics, military, and athletic GPAs, admissions closely evaluate a balance of grades, leadership, and physical fitness. From the highly competitive admissions and grading criteria, one can see that every graduate from the United States Military Academy proudly leaves with three distinct personae: scholar, warrior, athlete. And true to its form as an apolitical institution, the United States Military Academy strictly does not entertain the influence of nepotism, legacy, or donations that recently exposed the admissions process with other elite universities. US Congress reviews the highly transparent and meritocratic process each year. Honestly, after learning about today's competitive environment, I am not sure at all if I would be accepted again as a first-time applicant.

Nonetheless, I still like to say it's not about getting in to West Point—it's about getting out. Once a talented young kid crushes the SATs and gets into a top Ivy League school, it's more or less cruise control on the way to graduation. Not so at West Point. You have to earn that degree, and many fall by the wayside, not just because of the broad, highly demanding core curriculum in both liberal arts and sciences (six days a week) but also because of the intense afternoons, weekends, and summers of military training, in addition to highly competitive, year-round athletics. I had been a three-sport varsity athlete in high school—I walked onto the varsity soccer and cross-country running teams my senior year on a dare—and I had taken a full load of AP classes at one of the most notoriously ruthless and competitive Bay Area public high schools, but that was child's play compared to the rigors of West Point, where I was locked into an intense schedule from sunup to sundown. On top of that, we were held severely to a rigid Honor Code: a cadet may not lie, cheat, or steal, nor tolerate those who do.

My road to West Point had begun with a venal act of petty theft, pinching Gus Lee's book from a hippie bookstore. Lee had written about honor and duty. I had read the words, but I was about to learn the meaning of them.

WEST POINT, NY

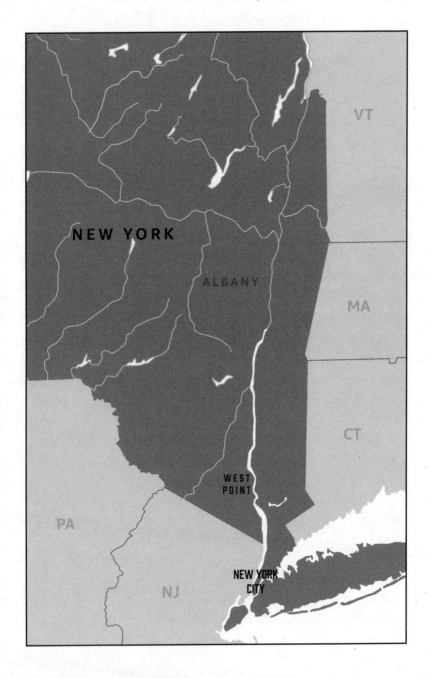

Chapter 4

Standing Eight

I study another picture from time to time, mostly when I need to remind myself of how many things have changed and how far I've come. It's a picture of my father and me on my twelfth birthday. I was alone in my room, and he came in, wished me a happy birthday, and hugged me. Over the next few years, a gulf would grow between us, fractures that would widen and then narrow. I suppose that's the experience of every father and son. But on that day, there was no distance between us at all. He told me that, according to the Chinese calendar, it was the Year of the Goat (Greatest of All Time!), just as it had been the year I was born. There would not be another for twelve more years. He urged me to imagine what I would be the next time the Year of the Goat rolled around. I tried. With all my heart. I looked into the mirror and tried to picture myself as a young man, but all I could see was a twelve-year-old boy's fantasy of what a man might be: tall, good looking, surrounded by adoring women, rich. I didn't know then that to see what I might become, I needed to look inside myself. I didn't realize that was what my father was telling me to do.

I sometimes think that my father and Gus Lee might have been friends, if they had ever met. They were very different men, of course. My father was from a Taiwanese generation and culture that saw its era of military conscription as something to be proud of. But it was never what they wanted for their own children. There's an old Chinese proverb that translates roughly as this: "You wouldn't use a piece of good iron to forge a nail, and you shouldn't waste a good man on soldiering." In our culture, military service was considered akin to spending time in a medium-security prison, and it was only with significant reluctance that my father and mother acceded to my desire to attend West Point.

I got my teeth kicked in at West Point, both figuratively and quite literally. I'm sure you'll have no difficulty guessing the figurative part. Here I was, a not particularly imposing Asian kid from sunny California, suddenly crammed into a gray uniform in an imposing gray citadel overlooking the Hudson River, surrounded by people as foreign to me at the time as the townspeople of Zaruma had been. As West Point awards fully funded appointments from all corners of the country, it tries to be as diverse and inclusive as it can. However, volunteering for the military adds a selective filter of its own, and the dominant culture is highly conservative, white, and rural, in style and tone, and this is reflected on a smaller scale even at an elite academic institution like West Point. I recall my southern classmates proudly flying their Confederate flags while taking photos with the statue of General Robert E. Lee, a famous top graduate, as both officers and cadets looked on either approvingly or without comment, which made me incredibly uncomfortable and confused.

There were very few Asians in the nineties, only 2 or 3 percent of the entire student body at West Point, particularly when compared to the Ivy League contemporaries, who accepted 20 percent Asians consistently year after year. Note the comparable University of California network of schools that accepted 40 percent Asians, unbridled by racially categorized affirmative action policies, nearly double the Ivies. The reverse effects of affirmative action have been a long-standing controversial and eyesore topic for high-performing Asian Americans, even harking back to my era of college applications, as Asians face much higher competition and standards for a limited number of spots due to our classification as a racial minority. In June 2023, the Supreme Court finally struck down affirmative action on the back of Asian American lawsuits against universities, and this is the first time I have ever felt in my life that our interests were heard on a political matter. While long overdue, it was a tremendous victory and a testament to the increased exposure Asians are receiving in pop culture and media today, in my opinion. But to be fair to West Point, there were also strong cultural reasons why fewer Asians elected to apply in the first place.

Interestingly, those Asians who were there were nearly all Koreans, products of a martial culture that had come to link West Point with General Douglas MacArthur, a major hero in the Korean War. MacArthur is arguably the greatest spokesperson for the academy of all time, crediting the Long Gray Line repeatedly in famous public speeches, and I'm sure he never thought that one of the most visible impacts of his efforts today would be an overwhelmingly dominant majority of Koreans in the Asian American population at the academy. There were four regiments of cadets in the organization at West Point, and sometimes both the Koreans and others would casually joke about a "fifth regiment" existing of the Koreans. Again, there were not many Asians, particularly to a kid like me who went to a high school that was over 50 percent Asian, but since we stuck out so much, oftentimes others would point out even just two or three of us standing near each other and make loud and uncomfortable jokes about wondering if the place was still actually the "United States" Military Academy.

Relatively speaking, I was pretty much the only me in my class. There were perhaps four or five other cadets with the same ethnic Chinese background in the entire school. It is a common misperception in America that simply because it is easier to categorize us all under a geographical umbrella term of "Asians," that we are culturally alike across the dozens of ethnicities. While I ended up gravitating toward the Koreans for a sense of protection, they have their own distinct, hierarchical form of norms and customs, and are ferociously proud of keeping to their traditions. Cupertino was mostly Chinese and Indian, and while similar in a few respects, like emphasis on education, prestige, and filial piety, it was an eye-opening cultural learning experience for me as I became fully immersed in its hierarchical nature as an active member of this close-knit Korean community at West Point. Indeed, this community influenced me later on to choose serving on the DMZ north of Seoul for two years as my first duty post, and I still lean heavily on my Korean network today for business and personal affairs.

I am always asked if there was racism at West Point toward Asians. There was casual prejudice toward all minorities at West Point in the late nineties, of course, and in a few minor quarters, there was a pervasive drumbeat of some outright racism, too, not terribly unlike any other university in that time period. But what was unique is that cadets held authority and power over each other under military law, and upperclassmen could say practically anything they wanted to plebes during my era, especially behind closed doors.

The few times that I encountered blatant racism was during plebe year, usually when we were not allowed to speak or look around freely, or even walk normally—we were required to "ping," or rapidly march at a pace of 120 steps per minute, which was tantamount to running everywhere—and we were subject to random hazing for eight months by upperclassmen more or less anytime they felt like it. A few times, a clique of gutless upperclassmen snuck up behind me while I was standing at attention and not allowed to move or look around, and whispered in my ear to go back to China, even though I had never been there. There was a time period of a few days that two upperclassmen decided that a Korean classmate and I looked absolutely identical, and they would order us into the hallways for hours to be paraded in front of their friends, calling others to come by to look at us as though we were zoo animals, laughing and pointing, while explaining as if they were anthropology professors that it was indeed true that all Asians looked alike. I was a head taller than my classmate and wore glasses—we did not look anything alike.

Those a little less overt in their casual racism talked to me as if I were a sort of specimen, as if they were engaging in some cross-cultural experiment to determine how "you people" celebrate Christmas or had better peripheral vision with our flat and slanted eyes. (I always replied, "Yes, I see much better than you do.") The most disturbing example of casual racism was the sexual fetishization of Asian women, and more than a few upperclassmen leeringly asked if it was true that Asian women had tighter, horizontal vaginas, followed immediately by a request to introduce them to my sister or my friends.

I did my best to ignore the slights and innuendos. I did not come to West Point to be the Martin Luther King Jr. of Asian cadets, and I learned to pick my battles. Primarily, I didn't have the capacity to worry about it, subtle or not, because I was barely surviving the day-to-day challenges regardless of these infrequent racial barbs.

I was doing everything I could just to stay afloat as a horribly inept plebe, and this attracted numerous upperclassmen and their worst sides like moths to a flame. Hazing me had nothing to do with my being Asian originally, but it gradually exposed the subconscious bias of certain upperclassmen, who associated my deficiencies with my race. Over time, I realized that they did not even understand their offhand comments were possibly offensive to me, which made it easier for me to ignore. However, their indifference is also reflective of the mild racism that Asians regularly face in America—we are not permitted to have any consideration for these matters as we are viewed subconsciously as foreigners by default. I learned from my plebe-year experiences where we lay in broader American society's view, which was previously masked to me in my little Asian bubble in Cupertino.

To be clear, there were plenty of other Asian classmates who likely did not see any of this if they were strong plebes, so this was not a common experience. This intense plebe-year experience led me to being a social ghost for the rest of my time at West Point, and I spent most of my time trying to get off campus to pretend to be anything but a cadet and be as Asian as possible, oftentimes traveling far distances to Asian student conferences at other universities. I hated being at West Point every single day for many reasons, including that it is essentially like living in a minimum-security prison, but like many of the other extreme challenges I took on in the Army, my Asian shame of failure did not allow me to quit no matter how miserable I was.

In a strange way, that low hum of antipathy and prejudice strengthened my resolve. I would eventually learn that if I wanted something bad enough, I had to be willing to take the hits to get it. If I was not willing to sacrifice in order to win, then it meant that I had never wanted it badly enough in the first place. While I would be lying if I said these experiences during plebe year at West Point did not bother me, the types of extreme hazing and suffering that I underwent later in my journey to US Army Special Forces made me wish all they did to us was utter a few racist remarks by comparison. If I let mean words, slights, or even obstacles stand in my way, then I probably wasn't hard enough to lead America's best in the first place on its most dangerous and complex missions.

As a Green Beret, I came to another profound understanding about identity in the military—being an elite warrior is a cultural identity all its own; it becomes the sum and substance of who you are. In the Green Berets, the Special Forces Operational Detachment Alpha (ODA) team-room environment is a legendary and sacrosanct space filled with the hardest, most cunning, and fiercest warriors that America offers. Though it does not always achieve perfection in practice, as we'll see later, once you're a Green Beret, that is your identity, your culture, and your heritage, whatever culture you came from. During my time there, racism was not an issue in the Special Forces because nobody cared who you had been. If anything, reacting to a racist joke or comment in the team room would highlight that you were not a special operator and teammate first—you were the color of your skin first. The only thing we cared about was competency, consistency, and commitment: whether you could pull your weight, and whether we could count on each other when bullets were flying and bombs were exploding all around our heads. They say there are no atheists in foxholes. I don't know if that's true, but I can tell you that there aren't a lot of bigots or "wokeness" down there. There are just fellow members of a sacred and special tribe who always put the mission and the team before themselves.

Looking back, I realize how poorly prepared I was for West Point. By any measure, even physically, I was probably one of the weakest cadets in both my "Beast Barracks," the nickname for West Point's summer boot camp before plebe year, and in my academic company, B-3 (still known today as "the Bandits"). Being a star high school tennis player may have done wonders for my hand-eye coordination, but when it came to feats of pure brawn, I came up short. I failed the first physical fitness test. Nothing that Francisco had taught me back in Cupertino prepared me for the forty-two push-ups in two minutes demanded of every cadet. My pathetic pecs were simply not up to the task. As a Green Beret ten years later, I could routinely do one hundred push-ups and barely break a sweat, with one man with his hand under my chest to check for the full range of the push-ups, and another man with his hand on my elbow to ensure full lockout. But not back then. Back then I was doomed to spend my entire first semester of daily wake-ups at 4:00 a.m. in the remedial class, doing extra physical fitness training with largely overweight cadets who had also failed the exam.

It would have been one thing if my shortcomings were merely physical. But they weren't. My comfortable, cosseted life in Cupertino, where my eccentricities had been tolerated if not condoned, left me psychologically unprepared for the rigors of West Point. I will never forget receiving our first grades at the end of plebe year and seeing that I was militarily ranked 1,198th out of 1,198 cadets. It was no wonder after failing nearly every military skills test during Beast and plebe year, like basic rifle marksmanship, land navigation, and even matters like room inspections or shining my shoes well enough. I was still shocked to see my name at the very bottom of the pile. You name it, and I failed it—everything and everyone around me felt entirely unnatural and out of place.

Admittedly, I was also a spoiled kid from South Bay when I arrived, and it showed. I had a malingerer's attitude, a sense of lazy entitlement, obvious enough to catch the attention of the upper-class cadets, who felt duty bound to wring every drop of slouching self-regard out of me. Those sneering upperclassmen targeted me for additional "training," a time-honored West Point euphemism for hazing, above and beyond the relentless regimen of academically challenging classes and the daily physical training and harsh discipline that began before dawn at zero-holy-shit-thirty and ended when you fell face-first at attention into your bunk.

The traditional West Point full year of plebe hazing formed in the 1800s is no longer in existence, and the class of 2001 is arguably one of the last classes to have endured the true, final remnants of a banished system. There was an openly concerted effort to truly change the school for its two hundredth anniversary class of 2002. Of course, every class at West Point famously refers to itself as the "last hard class," and classes before me certainly had it even harder, but the next three years of plebes were much more relaxed in my view. The Army formally (and correctly) began phasing out and discouraging these questionable hazing practices in 1990, but cadets initially refused to comply entirely, and most officers and professors, in particular the West Point graduates—called "Old Grads"—quietly disagreed and turned a blind eye for the most part.

By the time my plebe year of 1997 rolled around, undoubtedly hazing had significantly diminished, but it was still alive and well. The true hammer dropped in 1998 with officers suddenly and severely punishing upperclassmen for any form of hazing, when the Golden Class of 2002 arrived, the bicentennial class of West Point, a resentful point for my class, which essentially was the last class for everything that sucked, from our point of view. And despite the heavy frowning on hazing—I am not proud to admit this—I still paid this back in spades when I became an upperclassman, having received so much "training" on every tiny little West Point rule and detail. I was oftentimes alone in continuing the abusive cycle to the new plebes and willing to risk being punished out of indignation at the radical departure from my own experience.

After a very rough first year—I have a recurring nightmare, not of combat, but that I am a plebe covered in cold sweat again in those dimly lit hallways of Eisenhower Barracks being screamed at for hours on end—I finally made it to Recognition Day in the spring, a formal ceremony where the rest of the Corp of Cadets "recognize" the plebes as real humans, call us by our first names, and permit us to walk around and act normal again. But even in the final days, a particularly spiteful female upperclassman singled me out to harass me incessantly throughout the final weeks and up to the moment of recognition, as she had done all year in an impressively consistent manner.

When she rotated to stand in front of me during the ceremony, instead of shaking my hand, heartily pounding my chest, and congratulating me for making it through plebe year, like all the other former tormentors who had stopped harassing me months ago, she icily told me that under no circumstances would I ever successfully graduate from West Point, nor did I deserve to ever be a US Army officer. As humiliating as the eight long months of berating and criticism were, I always thought she was teaching me the way that West Point wanted her to and had my best interests at heart underneath her hard exterior—until that moment. She never spoke to me again, and the last time I saw her was when she graduated a few months later, one of the first cadets to walk onto the stage at Michie Stadium to receive her diploma. Despite the sting of her final words to me, I had finally made it on that wonderfully crisp New York spring evening, and happily choked on cheap Swisher Sweets cigars with my fellow Bandit plebes at the base of the George Washington statue, arms around each other and in tears. Plebe year nearly broke me, but I somehow emerged alive on the other side.

And then I experienced my first real defeat.

It happened in the boxing ring. In his novel *China Boy*, Gus Lee wrote beautifully and compellingly about the art of boxing. His semi-autobiographical protagonist, a lost Asian American street kid named

Kai Ting, finds himself targeted for violence pretty much every time he leaves his house, so he finds himself a boxing coach in a run-down gym in San Francisco's Chinatown district, and he learns to fight. In the end, he takes on all comers and pummels the bullies who had tried to terrorize him. I immediately identified with Kai Ting. His story resonated perfectly with my fragile teenage ego, and I irrationally assumed that when and if the time came to prove myself with my fists, I'd be able to do it with the same grace and power that Ting had demonstrated.

In their infinite wisdom, the higher minds who designed the curriculum at West Point, many moons ago, decided that at least four times, every incoming cadet would be required to step into a boxing ring and face off against a fellow cadet, with both their safety and their GPAs riding on the bouts. Theoretically, the idea is to distill combat to its most basic level, to develop the warrior mindset and habits. But I've always thought that there was another reason for it. You have a couple hundred plebes, most of them male (more recently, also female), most of them still in the throes of rampaging teen hormones, facing daily pressure that would make most first-year college students crumble, and with almost no sanctioned mechanism for releasing all their anger and frustration. So why not let them lace up a pair of boxing gloves and pound the living hell out of each other? What could go wrong?

Here's another picture from my past. It's the first day of boxing class. The instructor, a bulldog of a man with a perpetual sneer, welcomes us to the program, spitting phrases like "the nature of the beast" and "only the strong survive."

As far as actual instruction went, there really was none. He showed us the basic stance and muttered something about where to hold your left to slow the other guy's right before it sends your head flying over the turnbuckle like a line drive to left field, and then the fists flew. This would have been bad enough if the only thing trying to kill me was the bitter, angry, testosterone-poisoned cadet in the other corner. But the military, which will joyously spend tens of millions of dollars on the latest gadget, had to cut corners somewhere, so they'd saved a few bucks by keeping only the minimum number of gloves and protective headgear for each mandatory boxing class, which meant that by the time I stepped into the ring each day at fourth period, that gear had already been sweated and bled into by three other unfortunates. I would strap the sopping-wet headgear on and literally feel the mixture of different people's fresh sweat roll down my face and into my mouth. God only knows what diseases fermented in those things.

To say that I knew nothing about the combat sport of boxing would be an understatement. The problem was that I didn't know that I didn't know. There was one moment during my childhood when my mother—the same woman, I remind you, who had dragooned me into the safe sport of tennis—agreed, for reasons I still don't understand, to allow me to take a few Muay Thai kickboxing classes at a gym in nearby San Jose. It was a respected fight gym, but my training consisted of being told to go to the corner and kick and punch a bag a few times while the proprietors happily collected my fees and I just as happily went back to school and bragged about it.

I had really learned nothing except to look like I knew what I was doing, and I could fake it well enough that on a couple of occasions, the instructor noted that I seemed to have "good form." But few things are as dangerous as modest praise, which gives you a feeling of confidence that can get you into serious trouble. For most of the boxing course, it wasn't a problem. Then came the end of the term. As a final exam, we had to fight four graded bouts against four different opponents in a week. The instructor graded our performance, and, of course, we got extra points if we won. While we had gone comparatively easy on each other during the term—a mutual agreement to malinger negotiated in silence and only with eye contact—when it came to the exam, all of us were out for blood. Our grade depended on how well we acquitted ourselves in the ring, and nothing at West Point mattered as much as a grade.

And it didn't just matter to the poor plebes pummeling the living hell out of each other in the ring. Because there are so few ways to let off steam at West Point, the first-year boxing finals have become a kind of social event over the long and storied history of the academy. When you step into the ring for your finals, you have an audience: fellow plebes, upperclassmen, officers, your other instructors—hell, even the janitors drop what they're doing to watch. It's like fight night in Vegas, except everybody's poorly and identically dressed. It adds a sense of excitement to the event—I mean, nobody ever cheers at a chemistry exam—and honestly, the cheers of the crowd were kind of intoxicating, making some of us forget that we were not really all that great at boxing.

Because I had accidentally beguiled my instructor with my supposedly good form, I was judged—inaccurately—to be one of the better boxers in the class, so I was paired up for my first bout with a guy who really was a decent boxer. Frank Pera was a tough Filipino American kid from San Diego with bulging biceps who had clearly not had a mother who pushed him into taking up tennis. This guy had been in some real fights.

I remember a cheer going up when we stepped into the ring, which I now realize was for Frank, and which should have been a warning to me. I remember circling, popping him on the chin with a quick jab, thinking I had connected. And then I remember a look of anger rising in his eyes, which is pretty much the last thing I remember. I never even saw his overhand right coming amid the flurry of punches he unloaded. All I know is that my head snapped straight back, jagged shards of white light started raining from the ceiling like a phosphorus bomb, my legs turned to noodles, and I dropped to the canvas like a stone.

I spent the next two days in the hospital recovering from a severe concussion, diagnosed with a traumatic brain injury.

It was not just a loss. It was a humiliation.

At least that's the way I took it. If I had learned anything from Gus Lee's book, and from watching *Rocky* over and over again as a kid, it was this: it's not how hard a punch you can throw; it's how hard a punch you can take and get back up.

That summer, back in Cupertino, I made it my mission to get back up from that defeat. The first thing I needed was to change my thinking. In my culture, and in my family, it's not uncommon or unexpected for a parent to use a little bit of corporal punishment to keep a kid in line. It's generally pretty gentle: my mother had a trick whereby if I was acting up at the dinner table, she'd deftly flip her chopstick, leaving a little rounded nub between her index finger and her middle finger, and jab me in the forehead with it. It wasn't enough to leave any permanent damage, but it got the message across in an unmistakable way. When the going got tough, my dad would rap me in the face with a flaccid rabbit slap, a practice so common that the kids I grew up with jokingly referred to it simply as the "CBH"—the Chinese backhand. I discovered only recently that my parents rarely hit my sister. I always assumed we both were cuffed regularly for lying about practicing piano or skipping Chinese homework, but it appears that my sister somehow skipped that essential step in child development in the Yu household, and yet she seems none the worse for it. Go figure.

These petite punishments were not intended to inflict pain but to inflict shame. And they did. Long before I ever stepped into the ring at West Point, I had been carefully conditioned to interpret a hit as a deserved rebuke for something I had done. In order to become a boxer—let alone a warrior and a leader—I had to rewire myself to see a hit as an act of aggression, to which I was expected, in fact entitled, to respond with even greater force.

It took me months to reframe my thinking, and I still have to remind myself that I have the right, and in some cases the obligation, to respond to injuries done to me. Meanwhile, I had to learn the finer points of boxing.

Just as Kai Ting had done in Gus Lee's book, I sought out a trainer, an old boxing coach, and I worked with him tirelessly. Over countless hours I learned how to duck and weave, when to retreat and when to advance, how to hold back and tire out your opponent, how to take a hit (even a good one), and when to move in for the kill.

I'm sure my mother was aghast. This brutal sport ran counter to everything she had ever wanted for me. She could not imagine a place more different from a tennis court than that sweat swamp of a boxing gym. But she said nothing. Looking back, I suspect that she—and my father—never fully understood how desperately I needed to banish the spectral image of the emasculated, puny Asian male that haunts so many of us and was magnified to me by my plebe-year experience at West Point as I learned what the rest of America quietly thought of us. That particular specter never troubled either of them, and my parents never saw me in the ring. But they stood with me, if only from a distance. I suppose, at some level, they understood my need to succeed in the boxing ring, and that need probably came from them too. In the Army, "Be all you can be" is a motto. But in my childhood home, it was an article of faith.

I had an epiphany that summer. I had come to understand that West Point—in fact, the military in general—is and always has been a hierarchy of pain, a constant test of suffering. Dig deep, confront your fears, be more hard-core than the next guy, and you'll be respected. In the Army, Ranger School pushes men (and as of recently, women too) beyond their limits, and then rewards their success with the coveted black-and-gold tab sewn onto the soldier's left shoulder. At West Point, the Brigade Open Boxing Championship, the famed academy-wide boxing tournament, serves the same function, crowning winners and shaming losers for over a hundred years. Senator John McCain famously won the championship at Annapolis, albeit from a less prestigious military academy somewhere south of West Point.

By the time I returned to West Point, I was a better boxer. And I believe I was a better man. I had a goal: to recover—in my estimation—from my humiliating performance in the boxing ring. Having grasped a few fundamentals during the short summer break, and having confronted myself in the process, I was itching for a chance to prove myself. I joined the B-3 Bandits intramural boxing team, and with each bout I found myself getting better, faster, stronger, wiser, and wilier.

That is important. For all its brutality—and let's not kid ourselves, it is a brutal sport—boxing is not just a matter of strength, nor is it only a test of stamina. It is those things, of course. The ring is where hand-to-hand combat is the order of the day. But it's more than that. Boxing is a test of discipline, of the ability to take a hit and stay the course through fear, pain, and surprise. At its core, boxing is a martial art, not a sport. It's the art of understanding your own strengths and limitations and using both to your advantage. It's the art of respecting your opponent's strengths and minimizing them, of assessing their weaknesses and exploiting them. It's the art where timing beats speed, precision beats power, and leverage beats strength. The psychological discipline and fortitude I developed and honed in those long hours of training and sparring would serve me well for the rest of my life, and never more than during the rescue of Evelyn Chang.

But first I had to reclaim my status at West Point. And I did. In my "Firstie" (my senior year), I bested a formidable opponent to win the Brigade Open Boxing Championship, and for the first time at the academy, I stood atop the mountain, looking down at my peers rather than lying buried, layers underneath others, at the bottom, looking up. Not too many high-level athletes can recognize that tennis and boxing are similar sports; their physical movements and footwork are closely aligned, and individual self-reliance and mental fortitude are required to win in both arenas.

Winning the championship, particularly after such an ignominious start, began to give me real confidence. I had not only recovered from my earlier humiliation; I had excelled. And I had found comfort in the raw hardness of the ring. It was for me a place where I could take the full measure of myself, and I was proud of the man I was becoming, a man who had fought his way back from failure and had learned—the hard way—not to fear it. I had the drive, the determination, and the strength to fight my way back, to improve my chances on a second or third time around. Boxing gave me something to believe in that nobody could take away. I was starting to believe in myself. I had caught a glimpse of a chance to be the man I had always longed to become, as long as I stuck to it.

And my newfound confidence went beyond the canvas. After failing at every damned thing under the sun in my first two years at West Point, I hit the books with a reinvigorated fervor and focus that I never had in high school. I became singularly focused on my studies and ended up graduating in the top 5 percent of my class. I had the third-highest rank in my computer science class, and my parents beamed with pride when, at my graduation ceremony, I walked up to the stage time and time again to receive my accolades.

Out of almost twelve hundred cadets who started on the famed Registration Day at Michie Stadium, about nine hundred graduated into "butter-bar" lieutenants, so named for the single yellow bar of their rank insignia. That's a lot of wannabe heroes who went home with their tails tucked between their legs after all the fanfare that accompanies a son's or a daughter's appointment to the United States Military Academy, particularly in small towns. But I wouldn't shed a tear for them. Being separated from our class may have saved their lives, as we were the class of 9/11, graduating just a few short months before those planes hit the towers and the Pentagon, leading to twenty straight years of war and making us the longest continuous combat class in the history of West Point. As I say to kids yearning for the adventure of combat today, be careful what you wish for, as our part of the Long Gray Line is no stranger to the darkness.

For me, 9/11 radically changed my view toward my entire existence and mindset as a US Army officer. In the summer of 2001, my decisions were largely based on seeking an exciting overseas adventure for a few years and then heading back to where I belonged in Cupertino, hopefully in a cube farm somewhere happily programming for Apple's next cool music device. I watched with wide eyes as the Rangers combat-parachuted into Afghanistan on CNN under night-vision recording and seized airfields, and then I saw leaked photos of the Green Berets riding horseback, fiercely bearded and dressed entirely like the local mujahideen fighters, and the stories of how they infiltrated the country in small teams to link up with Northern Alliance warlords and went on to lead the overthrow of the Taliban in a matter of six months.

I took 9/11 very personally, as I loved New York City and spent many weekends pretending to be a normal college student there, just an hour's drive south of West Point, and I believed my government when they told me that weapons of mass destruction (WMD) existed in Iraq and were connected to this tragic event. I also believed that perhaps I had finally found a place where I could use the lifelong handicap of being a forever foreigner to my advantage in the culturally immersive approach of the Green Berets.

Most of all, even though I was already a sworn commissioned officer, 9/11 truly changed my mindset. I now became a real volunteer to defend my country rather than primarily using the experience for my own self-interest. Decades later, I'd reflect at how naive we all were to be used in the last twenty years to achieve less than nothing, and I still grapple with my role as a pawn in the War on Terror, as all veterans quietly do.

However, graduating from West Point remains the best day of my life. I'll confess that I felt great relief watching Thayer Gate disappear in my rearview mirror, with nothing but a summer of adventure ahead of me, but West Point had kept its promise. It had broken me down, just as Gus Lee told me it would, and it had given me the tools to rebuild myself into the man I needed to be. The job was not finished, of course. Maybe it never is.

FORT BRAGG, NC

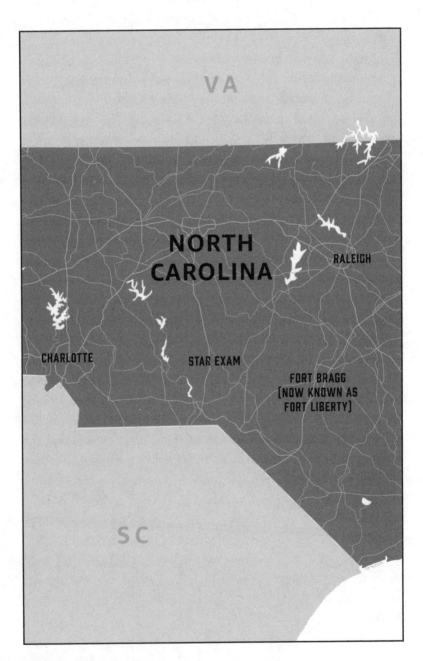

Chapter 5

Fallen Star

No longer the trench coat–wearing, greasy-haired punk from Cupertino, I was now Lieutenant Gene Yu. But I was also a bit of a robot, and an angry one at that, after my experiences at West Point. Anger is an occupational hazard for young officers, and my anger tainted my efforts as a young tank officer. I sometimes think the military cultivates it intentionally, that the grueling training and the sanctioned cruelty of hazing are designed not only to instill a sense of esprit de corps but also to inject just enough venom into your soul that your heart will be hard enough to do the dirty, soul-wrenching tasks demanded of soldiers on the battlefield.

My anger was more acute, and looking back, I realize that it may have been fanned by that dull drumbeat of subtle bias against Asians that I had experienced at West Point. If I'm to be totally honest, I have to admit that I had internalized some of it, that some part of me needed to prove that an Asian American officer could be every bit as gung ho as some blue-eyed farm boy from Arkansas. Maybe that's what prodded me to try out for Ranger School, fairly unusual for tank officers like myself.

It was the hardest physical challenge of my life to that point. At Fort Knox, where I attended the US Army's Armor Officer Course for about six months, we rose at 4:00 a.m. to run six to eight miles at a blistering pace, swim a few more miles, and then hurl ourselves onto the cold, damp bluegrass fields of Kentucky with muscle-tearing calisthenics, including hundreds of squats, lunges, and buddy-carry drills. To this day, even with all the training I've been through, nothing has been as physically demanding as pre–Ranger School training. With the volume of cardio we cranked out, for two hours straight every session, out of the eighty-eight aspiring lieutenants who first showed up, only sixteen were standing by the end of the course, and only eight were selected to attend Ranger School. I was the only one of them to graduate.

At Ranger School, I learned another powerful lesson about myself: I was tougher than I had ever imagined. Even as a boxer at West Point, I had never really thought of myself as tough. Athletic, yes. Smart. Tactical. Strategic. But I had never been that street fighter who barreled into the thick of the battle, gunning it out, blow for blow, in the pocket with my opponents. Instead I had cleverly lured them out, scoring against them with much better defense, technique, and hand speed.

And yet, somehow I found it in myself to power through the torturous, soul-crushing weight of it all, even as other men, guys who on the surface seemed far tougher than I, crumbled. I remember watching the broad shoulders of some blond, good old boy football-jock type heaving as he sobbed, frustrated and defeated, deep in the Georgia mountains after he'd raised his hand to quit. I've come to believe that my ability to tolerate high levels of pain and hard work is my superpower, and Ranger School taught me that it can translate into the physical realm as well.

Don't get me wrong, I had my moments of despair, too, both at Ranger School and later, when I survived—barely—the vastly more challenging Green Beret training, which was designed to either break you or make you stronger than you ever imagined you could be.

The worst failure for me was during an orienteering exercise in the godforsaken mountains of North Carolina for the Star Exam.

Perhaps more than any other exercise in Special Forces training, the Star Exam gets to the essence of what it means to be a special operator. It tests your resilience, your independence, your stamina, and your skills. When you're operating as a twelve-man A Team behind enemy lines, you must be able to work independently, and a large part of that independence relies on your ability to navigate through seemingly impassable terrain. Every major Western special forces "Selection" (or tryouts) dedicates a significant portion to examining your ability to navigate terrain. Why? For one reason, the exercise is a huge physical gut check. Another reason is that a special forces operator must always know where he is, particularly behind enemy lines. In fact, an oft-told Green Beret joke is that the first rule of being a Green Beret is always to look cool. The second rule is to always know where you are. The third rule is if you cannot abide by rule #2, make sure to abide by rule #1.

But also, since land navigation is an independent activity, it really tests a person's self-reliance and resourcefulness. More than a few times, the prospective operator finds his path blocked by what appears to be an insurmountable obstacle, like a broad river with a deadly current that on a map appears as a tiny creek, or a relief that shows a gentle dip in the terrain where in fact there is a cliff face. It is completely up to the operator to figure out how to persevere and get through the problem, because there is nobody around to help. You're entirely on your own. Whatever obstacles you encounter, you must overcome. And you have exactly twelve hours—to the nanosecond—to do it.

I'll confess that orienteering is not a skill I was particularly good at. Even at West Point, where land navigation exams are, by comparison, more like a kid's scavenger hunt than a life-or-death ordeal, I barely squeaked by and only after failing the first time. But I had committed myself—every fiber of myself—to being a Green Beret, and if that meant surviving the Star Exam, somehow I would find a way to do it.

I had no idea what was in store for me.

The Green Berets dump you in a trackless forest, somewhere in the piney nowhere at the outer fringes of the vast expanse of Fort Bragg, with a full pack, a dummy rifle, a map, and the Green Berets' very best wishes. You are instructed to find your way, in the allotted time, to a series of four checkpoints, scattered with gleeful randomness over thirty to forty square kilometers of staggeringly harsh terrain. Each checkpoint is revealed to you by a Special Forces instructor deeply camouflaged at the point in a small tent, once you find him, usually studiously reading a *Maxim* or *Playboy* magazine. The points crisscross over the vast training area to form the shape of a star once all four points are found, hence its name. Fail, and you're history.

It's not as if the Army doesn't understand the difficulty. At the time, the Star Exam was widely considered the most challenging land navigation exam in the US Army. In fact, even the best soldiers are expected to struggle with it, and so you get three chances, over three days, to complete the test. You pass if you get three points out of four on each of the three days, or you can be a rock star and get all four points in a single day. I was not a rock star. At Ranger School I had leaned heavily on supportive teammates on patrols, and the land navigation exam was far beneath the difficulty of the Star Exam. I just figured that, as I had done so many other times in my life, I could fake it until I made it, gutting it out for three points each day. As my Ranger instructors used to say to me when hinting I was doing something on patrol that was quite stupid or inefficient, "If you're not going to be a smart Ranger, you better be a tough Ranger then." I was usually the tough Ranger, unfortunately for me.

The Star Exam had other plans.

For the Green Berets, the Star Exam is conducted on some of the most baffling and challenging terrain in the continental United States. It's densely forested, and those who successfully complete the training spend the rest of their lives haunted by memories of the deep draws, the icy waters of Bones Fork Creek and Millstone Creek, edged with dense, thorny undergrowth that might as well be triple concertina barbed wire.

The topographical maps we were issued were from the 1980s and were unreliable, as the terrain had changed through decades of ecological growth and sedimentary shifts. Forget about any trails. This was not Google Maps, and there was no GPS. All we had were some barely perceptible squiggly lines and a lensatic compass.

It goes without saying that even when rudimentary trails did exist, we were not allowed to use them. The idea is that, as a Green Beret, when you're sneaking around behind enemy lines, you need to move in thick woods to conceal your movement from the bad guys. Obviously, it is much slower to tramp along through all the deadfall, especially in the dark of night under pouring, biting rain or snow, and Special Forces guys all remember shin bruises from slamming their legs into hard pine deadfall, or sliding ass- or headfirst into some gulch because they'd set a foot wrong.

And God forbid you use a red-tinted flashlight to see, except when buried under a camouflage poncho and plotting the next point's route on your map—immediate failure if caught by any of the dozens of Special Forces instructors roaming on ATVs on firebreak trails or sneaking around in the darkness with the Army's most advanced night-vision goggles to instantly spot you. You walk in the pitch-black darkness, and oftentimes all you can see is the lime-green glow of the lensatic compass's azimuth heading as you happily introduce your face to all manner of hard objects in the woods.

But the most critical difference between the Star Exam and any other land navigation exam in the Army is that you have to traverse this piney hell while carrying over sixty pounds of gear, a full battle load: ten-pound load-bearing vest, forty-five-pound backpack, and, most importantly, an eight-pound dummy rifle. This is a standard combat load for a two- or three-day patrol in the woods, but I'd be lying if I told you that it didn't make an already-torturous ordeal even more torturous, since candidates have already suffered through weeks of equally hard training on less than four hours' sleep each night. Sleep-deprived hallucinations and malnutrition were common. Indeed, that was the point. Only the strongest, the most prepared, could concentrate fully on their objective under such a burden. Only a real Green Beret could do it.

I failed my first time through the Star Exam, all three times I tried. And I did it in the most ignominious fashion.

It was Millstone Creek that did me in. The first two days, I had done well—not good enough, of course—but each day I had managed to reach three of my four objectives before the clock ran out. Except that on the second day, I realized I could not make it to the fourth point with only thirty minutes left and sat down to rest and recover a bit more for the next day. A nearby Special Forces instructor spotted me and decided I was not complying with the Star Exam by "quitting" and docked me a precious point, and now the one pathway to success that remained was to find all four points on the third and final day. Up to that point, I had made a Herculean effort to avoid the densest challenge, the dangerous no-man's-land around Millstone Creek, but facing the third day, I realized that if I was going to make it to all four checkpoints before time ran out, I was going to have to tackle Millstone Creek head-on.

It was do or die.

After three straight weeks of hacking through the woods, my feet were severely blistered—for all its claims of inclusiveness, the Army has never designed standard-issue boots that fit broad Asian feet—and my muscles were aching as I stumbled toward the banks of the creek. The brush was thick, so thick I could no longer just use my gloved hands to pick apart the branches and trees to make forward progress. With each step, the forest closed in behind me. And so I made an executive decision. I decided to strap my dummy rifle tight on the top of my rucksack, pull out my shovel, and start hacking at the foliage like I had a two-handed broadsword. I smugly applauded myself for having taken my issued shovel to a miller prior to Selection, requesting that it be especially sharpened to get around the rule that machetes were not allowed on the course.

After a couple of hours of struggling and hacking, inch by painful inch, I reached a thicker branch in the way of my progress. I thought about hacking around it, but then I peeked through the branches and saw that I was only about fifteen meters from the end of the thicket. The terrain began sloping upward, meaning the draw was coming to an end. I'd be coming back up to higher ground, out of the depths of Millstone Creek. I had already crossed the creek itself, wading through knee-high icy waters. My blistered feet were sopping wet, and I could feel the skin on them tearing with every step. I needed to get to somewhere I could sit to change into dry socks and dry boots, which I carried in my pack. So I decided to keep going, slashing away at the recalcitrant branch with every ounce of my strength. And just as it was about to give way, my shovel slipped in my hand and buried itself deep into my leg, its knife-like blade easily penetrating my flesh. I let out an animalistic scream as I looked down and saw the shovel protruding from my shin. I was so loud that later that night, a friend who had been at least half a mile away said he heard the cry and assumed it was a wounded wild animal.

It took me several minutes—several precious minutes—to overcome the shock and pain, paw through my backpack, fish out a T-shirt, and fashion a rudimentary bandage to sop up the blood. And then I pushed on.

In a way, I was proud of myself, and when I finally limped out of the thicket, I sat down next to a tree, breathed a huge sigh of relief, and fully tended to my wound. I changed out of my wet socks and tried to dry my feet with Gold Bond foot powder, an infantryman's second-best friend, but I suddenly realized that I had lost an infantryman's very best friend. My rifle was not strapped to the top of my pack. It was gone.

Somehow, while I was whaling away at the undergrowth with my makeshift machete, it must have slipped from my pack. This wasn't a minor slipup; this was a catastrophe. A lot of armchair warriors will tell you that this or that is the first rule of combat, but I'll tell you that the real first rule of combat is *Don't lose your goddamned rifle*. I panicked. I'll admit it. I limped back to the edge of the undergrowth, the remorseless terrain I had just traversed, and frantically searched for it. But it was gone. And with it, my dream of becoming a Green Beret.

Defeated, I reached down to retrieve my map and plot a new route back to the base camp to report that I had failed. But when I reached into my cargo pocket, my hand came out the bottom. Adding insult to injury, Millstone Creek's crown of thorns had torn out the bottom, and I didn't even have a map anymore. I literally had no idea where I was, or even which direction I should face to get back to base camp. I think I wept. I know I pounded the ground in frustration. Days in the woods, with all the physical pain I had gone through, had all come down to this. Not only had I humiliated myself by losing my weapon, but now I didn't even have a map—*on a land navigation exam.* Without a real plan, I listlessly grabbed my pack, and it was just luck that after an hour or so of mindless wandering, I walked directly into the Star Exam base camp.

Daylight was breaking, and I went up to the instructors' hut and knocked. One of the nicer Special Forces instructors came out with the steam rising from a fresh coffee mug and asked what I wanted; the Star Exam was only half-over. I sadly explained that I had lost my rifle and map, expecting him to laugh, spit in my face, and tell me to go wait in the "Quitter's Corral," a roped-off area where quitters sit in front of everybody in über-humiliating fashion. But he looked around, saw nobody, and told me that he thought I was a good candidate, that I had demonstrated strong teamwork and leadership the past few weeks. He had been watching me and was hoping that I would pass Selection despite the fact that I was an officer. Then he grabbed me another rifle and map and told me to continue.

Given a new lease on life, I quickly plotted my way back to the original point that I had tried to find. And then I ran. Injured and exhausted, with sixty pounds jostling around on my back, I limped, painfully, as fast as I could. I just ignored the pain as well as I could, and I *ran*, hoping for the best. I needed to get lucky, and I threw caution to the wind, moving with a maximum sense of urgency. The clock was ticking. I had only about four hours left to find three more points, and I was going to give it everything I had. I made it to my next two points within two hours, a pure stroke of luck buoying my spirits. I had one more point to hit. It was eight kilometers away, but thankfully there were no major obstacles in my path, no deep draws or malevolent creek beds to swallow me alive. Summoning every ounce of strength I had, I pushed on. I stumbled several times along the way, falling and reopening the wound on my left leg, but I didn't care. I wanted to be a Green Beret, and I was giving it everything I had.

With only a few minutes left, unable to locate the last point and circling the area over and over, in a last-ditch effort to find and cross the finish line, I dropped my pack, rifle, and gear and scrambled to the top of a tree, which of course is not allowed, but I was desperate. I could see my final objective. The Special Forces instructor posted there was serendipitously taking a leak, and I spotted the camouflaged point. The end was within reach, only about one hundred yards away. I quickly scampered to the ground, and with a huge smile, I strapped on my pack, grabbed my rifle, and started limping as fast as I could.

I was within one hundred feet of the instructor when he saw me, glanced at his timer, and coldly barked, "Time's already up! Sit down, Candidate."

FORT BENNING, GA

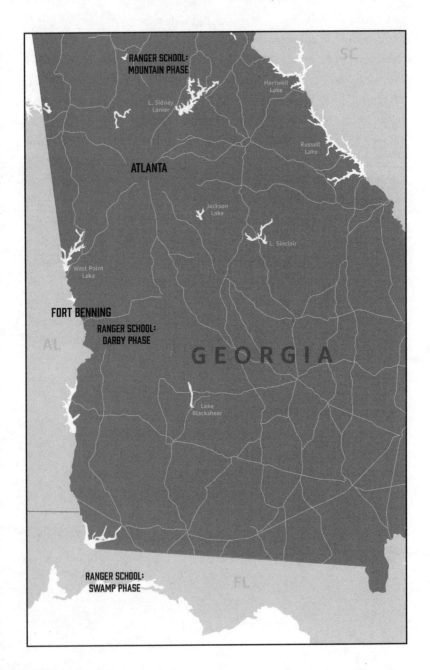

Chapter 6

The Ranger Creed

Another picture I sometimes reflect upon is unlike the others in my mental album. It's not a picture of me. But then again, maybe it is.

His name was Chang, no relation to Evelyn, the kidnapped woman. Chang is a common name, though Chang was an uncommon man: coincidentally a Taiwanese immigrant, relentlessly cheerful, if a bit awkward and generally inept. I first observed him in February 2002, during Ranger School. The training was rigorous, and it taxed me. It taxed Chang even more.

By the time I met him, he had failed the training six times. He had spent several months already struggling to pass the various initial tests at Ranger School, "recycling," or repeating, one of the three torturous phases of the infamous course, over and over, with no sign that he was ever going to succeed. And yet his leadership at the 3rd Infantry Division was in no hurry to bring him back. They were perfectly content to let Chang continue to fail Ranger School indefinitely. Most units would have pulled him out, at least after the second or third failure. As an officer, I certainly would not have allowed one of my own soldiers to damage himself like that for months on end as the prolonged sleep, food, and warmth deprivation undoubtedly harmed our health. It is common for Ranger students to have their core temperature drop to the low nineties in Fahrenheit degrees during the course and lose thirty to forty pounds as a result of malnutrition, like I did, let alone the psychological toll from less than four hours of sleep day after day. General human rights issues aside, I also bristled at how they were mocking him to his face with racist barbs, but like my plebe year at West Point, I was busy dealing with my own problems, trying to keep my head above water.

For some, I suppose, this bumbling little Asian man with a thick accent and an overabundance of enthusiasm might have been a laughingstock. But not to me or most of our classmates. To us, Chang was inspiring. We woke up each day unsure if we would make it through to the evening, even more fatigued from lack of sleep and food deprivation than the previous day, and this man had been there already for six months straight. He was a full-time professional Ranger School student for all intents and purposes. Even some of the instructors—hard, sometimes sadistic men—saw the spark of something special in this odd man, and although they incessantly tortured him, we could see that they begrudgingly respected him from time to time. Despite his failures, he would always pick himself up, brush off the dust, and throw himself right back into the fray, tackling every challenge, no matter how harsh or mundane, with the same gritty commitment. Chang was all heart.

Before each of the two daily meals during "City Week" of Ranger School, the first week aptly named as it is held on the garrison of Fort Benning before heading into the deep and remote Georgia woodland forest and mountains—which consists of massive amounts of physical hazing and painful training exercises conducted on four hours of sleep, designed to weed out the quitters—all the students line up in formation. Six are randomly selected to recite the Ranger Creed from memory. It is a requirement that, prior to arrival, candidates memorize the lengthy, six-stanza Ranger Creed. During training, as an individual student screams each phrase of the it, the rest of the Ranger class screams it back in thunderous repetition. If a candidate so much as stumbles on a single word, the entire class of two hundred or so is ordered to drop for a painful round of hundreds of cadenced push-ups and flutter kicks as the famously vicious Ranger instructors scream and spit expletives and hate-filled vitriol inches from their faces. And then they start the entire Ranger Creed again, from the beginning. Before some meals, we were stuck for hours trying to get through it in the freezing cold, with snow flurries falling around us. I realize now that it was all planned and staged, as part of the City Week hazing—there was never any intention or expectation of us successfully reciting the creed and allowing us to eat without punishment. At the time, though, we saw it as just one more link in an unbroken chain of torments. Even when we were allowed to eat, the Ranger instructors chased us in the mess hall, screaming inches from our faces to hurry up while we shoveled food into our mouths. Before we could get to all of those lovely meals inside, our stomachs turned with acid, burning us with the deep, soul-wrenching agony of hunger. We prayed each time to finish the Ranger Creed quickly so that we could eat, and the false hope just made the pain even worse.

At the beginning, by design, our class could not get through the Ranger Creed. We failed at every meal, which was twice a day. Eventually the Ranger instructors would decide enough was enough. They laughed derisively, called out Chang, brought him to the front of the formation, and made him recite the creed in its entirety alone. From the beginning stanza ("Recognizing that I volunteered as a Ranger") to the final line ("Readily will I display the intestinal fortitude required to fight on to the Ranger objective and complete the mission though I be the lone survivor"), Chang screamed himself hoarse in his heavy

Taiwanese accent, reciting each word, *with tears pouring down his face.* Chang believed in the Ranger Creed, to the very last word, and it was truly inspiring to all of us, fellow suffering Ranger students, to see how badly we all wanted to meet the challenge personified in his emotional display.

I never knew anyone who wanted anything as badly as Chang wanted to be a Ranger. He just couldn't pass the graded infantry patrols and he never made it out of Darby Phase, the first phase of Ranger School. He wasn't a very good soldier by most conventional standards, but there was something about him—his courage, his optimism, his hunger—that made the soldiers around him better. He was willing to give the final measure to get the job done. Ultimately, when I think about Chang, I see that he really embodied the soul of the Ranger Creed: to be willing to "fight on to the Ranger objective and complete the mission though I be the lone survivor." He knew what it means to truly give your all, your everything, and I am a stronger man—a stronger soldier—for having observed him. I know I haven't tried my best until I've showed up the way Chang showed up at Ranger School each day. The last time I saw Chang was when I was out-processing Ranger School three months later, and my graduating classmates and I walked past the mess hall where Chang was once again, in front of yet another new class, screaming the Ranger Creed.

I don't remember for certain, but I believe I conjured that image of Chang, passionately reciting the Ranger Creed, when I made the decision to return to Fort Bragg and subject myself to the horrors of Selection and the Star Exam a second time. I know I thought of him when I finally succeeded and became a Green Beret. And I can say with certainty that I've thought of him many times in the years since, every time I face a seemingly insurmountable obstacle. Whenever the road ahead of me seemed hard, too hard, it was Chang telling me what I needed to do, to fight on to the Ranger objective, though I be the lone survivor.

Years later, when I feared that we might lose Evelyn Chang, somewhere deep inside me, the image of Private Chang reciting the sacred words of the Ranger Creed urged me to keep up the fight.

HONG KONG SAR, CHINA

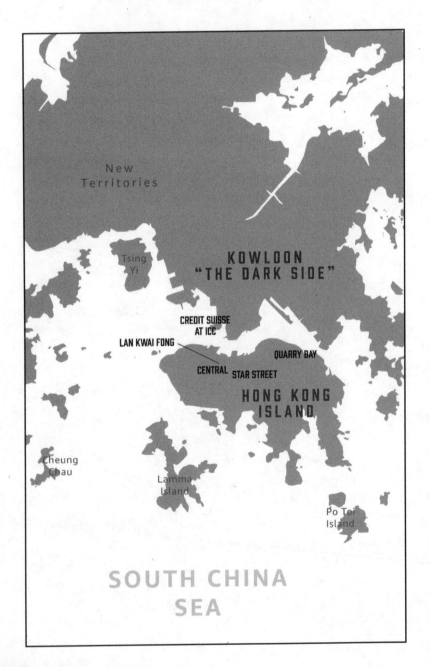

Chapter 7

Mother, May I?

It was hot and loud and crowded. The night air stank of frying fish, perfumed with the pheromones of other people's ambitions, and I just couldn't find the strength to take one more goddamned step. So I dropped my parcels—all the worldly possessions I could carry—and let myself sink slowly to the pavement as a sea of midlevel functionaries chasing pretty, petty dreams on the sidewalks of Hong Kong washed over me.

Years had passed since I was that lost boy in Cupertino, and more than a decade since I had proved myself at West Point and then on the battlefields in the War on Terror. It seemed like a lifetime since I had left the military in a moment of anger, and now here I was again, right back where I started, a lost boy, a forever foreigner down on his luck in somebody else's country.

It had all happened so fast. In just a matter of weeks, I had gone from the top of the world to rock bottom.

If you had seen me on this street eight weeks earlier, you could have read my résumé in my swagger. I was a top West Point graduate and a decorated Green Beret officer who had seen combat all over the world. Then, through skill and cunning, I had worked my way to the top of the food chain with a front-office trading-floor seat in the cutthroat world of international finance. I had leveraged that into a cushy sinecure in the Asia operations of one of Silicon Valley's darling start-ups. I had even impressed myself. More importantly, I had almost impressed my mother.

And yet there I was, practically curled up in the fetal position, a nobody. I had again become that kid I used to be: the Asian kid in a frigid sea of flinty white faces in Concord, Massachusetts; the kid who used to snap to attention twice a day and intone the Pledge of Allegiance in a New England drawl, just to prove that he could fit in; and the awkward high school eccentric in the wealthy promised land of Cupertino, California, a greasy-haired misfit, Asian to the core but still just a little too American to blend in with all the obedient, ambitious, and respectful Asian kids in Silicon Valley.

My whole life is a story of second chances. I got a second chance at West Point after finishing plebe year militarily ranked the lowest in my class, a chance to redeem myself after my humiliating performance as a plebe boxer. I got a second chance from the Army, not known for its compassion, when I was allowed to master the Star Exam after my dismal first attempt. I trained for six months on weekends while stationed at Fort Benning, Georgia, simulating the Star Exam, and when I returned, I completed four points on the first day, entirely before daybreak, with the fastest time of my entire class. Time and again, throughout my life, I had stumbled across some way to turn a defeat into a win.

I like to think of the sniper's world as a metaphor for this idea of succeeding after the first attempt. The unofficial sniper motto is "One shot, one kill," but I learned as a student at US Army Sniper School that the true hallmark of a great sniper team is not whether they hit the target on the first shot but rather the second shot. The spotter next to the sniper helps immediately adjust the windage and elevation based on where the first shot missed, in order to bring the sniper on target for the second shot. Hitting the target on the first shot is, frankly, pure luck, since it is impossible to know exactly how the wind, the distance, and even the temperature will affect the trajectory of the bullet's pathway over a long distance. It's the speed and accuracy of the second shot that marks how good the sniper team really is after a quick adjustment. I like to think of my life of second chances in this manner, as I've always believed my real skill resided in the second shot, rather than giving up when I did not get lucky on the first.

There's a story about me, now part of the lore of the Green Berets, that illustrates this. During a survival training exercise in which a team I was leading was supposed to be living off the land, trying to evade capture from dog-tracking teams, we stumbled into a clearing where, in the distance, we could see a small group of men, whom I later learned were Central American meth cookers relocated to the American South. We were surprised to see them, and they were probably even more surprised to see us, a band of emaciated, filthy men emerging from the tree line. My men and I hadn't eaten in seven days—our last bite had been a partially decomposed dog we had found floating in a river with a bullet lodged in its chest—and by the time we found the meth dealers, the woods were fresh out of dead dogs. So I made an executive decision. I approached the oldest of the meth cookers and, using the Spanish I had honed during that Ecuadoran summer back in high school, I persuaded him to drive me twenty miles in his beat-up pickup truck to the nearest town of Aberdeen, where, using a memorized credit card number, I ordered a dozen pizzas and brought them back to my men.

When word got out about what is now the well-known Green Beret story of the "Pizza Guy," the Army was predictably unimpressed, and I nearly washed out of training. But once again, I was given a second chance. Maybe they figured that even if I hadn't followed the letter of the law regarding proper foraging and survival behind enemy lines, I had followed the spirit of it. To this day, I believe that an officer's chief responsibility is to care for, provide for, and protect his men, using all the tools at his disposal, and if he can do that with extra pepperoni and cheese, it's his solemn duty to do so.

After much deliberation, my superiors allowed me to return for a winter Survival, Evasion, Resistance and Escape (SERE) course, which was unheard of, and they also decided to punish me by placing me on "probation" and sending me to serve indefinitely as a spare staff officer in the southern Philippine jungle (instead of the traditional direct route to an A Team for newly minted Green Beret captains), where we were combat-advising the Filipino military in their fight with Abu Sayyaf, the Al-Qaeda–linked organization discussed at the beginning.

It was a trial by fire. By an odd twist of events, I found myself the de facto battle captain of an operations center advising over five hundred Filipino soldiers and marines as they jointly attacked Jolo Island, with the intent to destroy Abu Sayyaf once and for all. We failed. But I acquitted myself well enough that not only was I released from purgatory; I was also given the pick of teams to lead. I chose the only one that would take me to the front lines in Iraq from the Okinawa-based unit. Suffice it to say that the time I spent in the Philippines—much of it on the very same island where Evelyn Chang would be held eight years later, fighting the same people who would kidnap her—gave me insights and skills that would prove invaluable.

I respected myself, and the Army respected me. I was laterally promoted into one of the five regional counterterrorist units and graduated from the highest-level close quarters combat shooting and hostage-rescue operator course the US Army Special Forces offers, obscurely called the Special Forces Target Acquisition and Exploitation Techniques and Tactics Course, at Fort Bragg's legendary Range 37 compound. I jumped and parachuted out of just about every type of fixed- or rotary-wing aircraft in the US military's inventory—even hot-air balloons in Korea and Thailand. In Iraq, I ran nightly missions into the hell that was Baghdad's Sadr City, and I did it with the best of the best.

When I returned from my fourth combat deployment in Iraq—as one of the most deployed captains in my year group, forty out of forty-eight months—I was selected for early promotion to major, one of only nine Special Forces captains in the entire US Army to be accorded that distinction. It was a hell of an honor for a kid who used to salute the flag twice a day back in the place where the United States was born. It was the culmination of all I had been working for ever since I'd tried to lift my battered head from the canvas in that ring at West Point, a grand go-to-hell gesture to all the haters and the doubters who saw me as soft and weak and not fit for duty, let alone leadership. Most of all, it was a gift to the younger me, the kid who had no role model to look up to, a man who went against the stereotypes. I had struggled. I had failed. I had tried again, and against all odds, I had made it.

But that victory was short lived. Maybe it was my own insecurity, or maybe that subtle bias I remembered from West Point was playing tricks on my mind, but just as my military career was about to reach the next level, rumors about my relationship with my uncle—the President of Taiwan, a man I barely knew—began to arise. These rumors had career implications. After risking my life and proving myself on battlefields from Iraq to Kurdistan to the Philippines, suddenly my loyalty to the United States was being questioned. I answered the Army's questions and insinuations honestly and directly, banishing whatever doubts they may have had, but the experience left me confused and bitter, and at the age of thirty, having done nothing else with my adult life except serve my country, I left the Army, honorably discharged but angry that my honor had been called into question nonetheless.

I did a stint at grad school—a prestigious one, of course. And when, inevitably, I got bored with that, I drifted into the world of high finance. Again, it was utterly accidental. An old buddy from my days in Seoul, a three-hundred-pound Korean American jiujitsu instructor named Henry Jung who was, unbeknownst to me at the time, secretly a wealthy investment banker by day, introduced me to a friend of his. Such is the world of high finance. The friend, Matt Pecot, was then head of prime services in Asia for the international banking firm Credit Suisse (RIP). Underneath that $3,000 suit, though, Matt was a kindred spirit. Not only was he a former Green Beret officer; he had, in fact, commanded the same counterterrorist team in Okinawa seventeen years before I had. And like me, he had been one of the very few US Army Special Forces captains selected early for promotion to major.

Within five minutes of studying my bona fides, Matt presented me with a chance to change my life—forever, he suggested—by offering a path that led directly to an open front-office equity swaps trading seat in the Hong Kong headquarters. I looked at the compensation number he showed me and immediately packed my bags. I showed up for duty the next week at Credit Suisse, inspired by Matt's rare example, and radically altered the trajectory of my life away from the pathway of national service that West Point had so carefully institutionalized into me. The downside was that I would forever be a grad school dropout, to the great disappointment of my parents. But the pay package helped salve my sense of grief over their disapproval.

I started, of course, at the bottom. But the bottom at Credit Suisse is a bit higher than the bottom elsewhere. I was reluctant to start full time, as I was too embarrassed to share that I did not exactly know the difference between an investment bank and a commercial bank, so Matt offered me a summer internship to help me figure it out. That internship came with a $30,000 paycheck, plus travel and hotels, and a chance to stand inside the beating heart of Wall Street. I jumped at the opportunity.

I was one of many. Most of the interns were just kids, wunderkinds from Harvard or Wharton with big dreams of breaking into the world of high finance. I was only thirty-two, but to them, I seemed ancient. They called me Uncle Gene. Like interns anywhere, we were treated with indifference at best, and occasionally with borderline contempt. More than once, a trader would demand that an intern fetch him a bone-dry cappuccino, and the Harvard and Wharton boys and girls would recoil. Not me.

If my years in the military had taught me anything, it was that if you first make yourself useful, you can sometimes leverage that to make yourself indispensable. And this was the same rite of passage in any organization that considers itself elite—hazing. I had already earned a PhD in being hazed and, later on, in hazing others, in whatever shape or form, and this was a huge joke to me. The young hotshots became flustered by it all on the trading floor, and I chuckled to myself, finally finding a small advantage over all the finance wizardry they had freshly learned from their universities.

"You want that with almond milk?" I asked, before jogging off to fetch the young man his coffee. I enjoyed a leisurely stroll through the iconic International Finance Centre mall in Hong Kong, stopped by a bookstore or two, a welcome escape from the awkwardness and humiliation that was the lot of my fellow interns, standing around along the wall of the Exchange Square trading floor with their hands in their pockets.

It didn't take long to parlay that temporary servitude into something more substantial, and soon I had a sense of curiosity that perhaps I was bound for a full-time, long-term career in the big-buck universe of Wall Street, despite my previous convictions of service imbued into me from my time in uniform. I quickly dispatched any misconceptions about my being an obsequious coffee boy one morning after a drunken night out with my coworkers, a mix of Brits, Aussies, and both local and overseas-born Asians like me, a typical makeup of backgrounds in a top-tier bulge-bracket investment bank in Hong Kong. It was my third day on the Credit Suisse equity swaps desk, the team of prime brokers that lend stocks to the top hedge funds and places their short trades in the Asia markets on their behalf, and all the hotshot finance guys and girls could talk about was Asphodel, the first-ever CrossFit gym in Quarry Bay, on the east side of Hong Kong Island. The place offered a 5:00 a.m. class just for the alpha bros and sisters of the high-finance world, and pretty much half the desk had signed up so they could get to work by six thirty. The night before, the other half had grown tired of hearing people ask me about my time in the military and challenged me to join them for a drink in the Lan Kwai Fong bar area, the famous epicenter of Hong Kong expat nightlife, perhaps to see if I could talk about anything else. That drink turned into two, which turned into three, which became a bender that lasted until last call in the early hours of the morning in Kowloon, which expats call the "Dark Side," the more local area of the territory across from Hong Kong Island, where most of those in the finance industry lived and worked. Hong Kong, in the heady days before and after the 1997 handover to China, had a reputation for a great many things, not least as a place where people worked hard and partied harder.

Needless to say, that 5:00 a.m. class at the CrossFit box was a challenging ordeal, particularly for those newly recruited by Charlie Pratt, one of the leading senior equity sales traders. But not for me. I guess they hadn't realized that CrossFit had been adopted early by Green Berets and SEALs, that I had been practicing it for at least five years, and that, as a former special forces operator, I had experience flogging my body to unimaginable extremes after subjecting myself to far greater abuse than a night of drinking, although I'll confess that we drank our share on missions all over Southeast Asia when we had a bit of downtime. Nobody from the previous night of drinking even pretended they were going to show up.

I didn't think I performed particularly well in the workout after just two hours of fitful sleep, but the fresh and well-rested senior traders I'd left sufficiently in the dust certainly thought so. In retrospect, maybe I should have been more grateful to the sadists at Ranger School for teaching me how to force myself awake and will myself into action through the muddy lethargy after a night of insufficient sleep.

My colleagues were in awe. "Gene drank half of us under the table last night, and then killed the other half at CrossFit!"

The military and the world of global finance share more than just a killer instinct, though that's useful in both endeavors. Few workplaces can claim to rival the sharklike culture of a US Army Special Forces team room, but an investment bank's trading floor certainly gives it a run for the money. They also share an almost-blind devotion to the outdated notion of virility, a very retro reverence for the hard-drinking, hardworking tough guy who can close a bar, sweat out the booze, and then take on the world and look good doing it. The argument is that it is an important broker skill to drink all night and still make it to the desk on time to place the incoming trades first thing in the morning now that you're BFFs with the hedge fund client. My first introduction to the other side of Wall Street trading floor culture was one Friday morning after the big weekly "Client's Night." I was in the men's bathroom, where I naively thought to wipe up a small pile of spilled white soap powder on a sink and greatly angered an exhausted senior trader who had popped into a stall temporarily. Regardless, the hypermasculine alpha culture of the old-school trading floor places a great deal of weight on these "skills," and after overhearing this episode of Drunken CrossFit Kung Fu, my "desk head" managing director gave me the full-time offer just three days into the internship, unaware that Matt had already offered me the job or that I was barely standing that day.

I now had everything, or so it seemed. I had a full-time job with good pay and a certain level of prestige. I had more money in my pocket than I'd ever had in my life, and everywhere I went in Hong Kong, I was spreading cash like Henry Hill in *Goodfellas*. I was treated with a respect bordering on deference. My parents even asked me, once, for stock tips, subtly admitting that I may have finally learned something of value that they did not already know.

I had won the affection of the kind of woman I had fantasized about when I was a boy back in Cupertino—a flamboyant, volatile, passionate young woman from a successful family, a true Asian American princess and former Miss San Francisco with a restless soul and an admirable sense of adventure. She was remarkable. An entrepreneur in her own right, she had left home, set up shop in a dismal factory town in China, and was now manufacturing her own line of specialty competition cheerleading outfits for American high schools.

Our relationship was fraught. We argued often, and bitterly, but when we weren't fighting, we had a lot of fun together. On paper, I should have been happy. I should have been content, at least. But I

wasn't. Maybe, back then, I could not have been. I had become institutionalized by the Army, and I struggled to adapt to the world I'd
voluntarily left behind.

The old angst, the old impatience, the old frustration began to
return once the initial excitement of having money for the first time
wore off, and the hedonistic adaptation settled into my life. There was
nothing meaningful to me about working in an investment bank, putting in sixty-to-seventy-hour weeks helping wealthy people become
even wealthier. I began to see not my successes but a kind of bondage:
twelve hours a day staring at four computer screens, moving tens of
millions of dollars of other people's money around the globe, fighting
with my girlfriend, drinking my face off, working out, and then doing
it all over again at the break of each dawn.

I had the life and career opportunity that many dreamed of. And I
was growing to hate it.

I began to dabble more in the industry of mixed martial arts
(MMA) and created an apparel company in my free time called FLOW
into which I invested all my savings. We sponsored fighters at the local
Hong Kong MMA promotion called Legend Fighting Championships,
and one day, the founders asked me to be a referee when I was sitting in
the crowd because a travel issue had prevented the actual referee from
making it to the event. Turned out I wasn't halfway bad at the job,
and I ended up being a professional MMA referee on the side, further
trying to dull the lack of meaning in my professional life. But it was
not enough to replace the sense of purpose I'd had when I was a Green
Beret, not by a country mile.

I was offered the opportunity to spend the summer at a Credit
Suisse training program in New York. I was granted access to a mag-
nificent corporate apartment on Fifty-Sixth Street, a few blocks away
from Central Park. I spent most of that summer partying, but in my
defense, the training was intended for incoming associates, and I had
already been handling all of Credit Suisse's stock lending to hedge fund
clients for the Taiwan market, having stepped into the opportunity as

the only remaining business-level Chinese speaker in our team when the previous trader was poached abruptly. Not exactly titillating work, even for traders, but I knew my job, and the training had zero to do with it—it bored me to tears.

In hindsight, it was one of the best summers of my life. I caught up with an old friend and fellow B-3 Bandit from West Point who was working in finance as well as at Morgan Stanley named Michael Lavalle, and I confessed to him that my seemingly perfect life in Hong Kong was anything but. His partner, Suzanne Xie, suggested that I investigate the opportunities at Palantir Technologies, a hot new tech security and government services "big data" start-up in Silicon Valley.

To my utter surprise, this company, which at the time purportedly rejected an incredulous 99 percent of its applicants, hired me, and I immediately notified my colleagues at Credit Suisse that I wasn't coming back. I then managed to persuade the powers that be at Palantir to send me to Singapore to help start up the Asia office. And once again, it seemed that I was back on top.

After a year of working with amazingly intelligent colleagues and learning what true, fast-moving Silicon Valley culture looked like, the axe fell. I'm still not really sure what happened. Maybe it was them. Maybe it was me. Maybe the company's growing pains and my own didn't quite sync up. The bottom line was that I was unemployed for the first time in my life, and I got my first dash of the cold reality that employment and financial security often have nothing to do with your competence, or skill, or anything in your control.

I realized that the world was split into two categories. There were the people who stepped on the playing field and made their own way, and there were the people who worked for them. If I wanted to be my own man and have real financial security, I needed to go my own way.

But I had no idea what that way might be. All I knew was that I had become the lost and confused kid from Cupertino again, adrift without any identity and entirely unsure what to do next. It was one of the lowest points of my life, and once again I peered into the abyss. I thought I was proving the universe wrong that the only thing I could be was a Green Beret with my early private-sector successes. Everything I thought I had built after my abrupt separation from the military had come crashing down around me, making me realize that I was the greater fool, after all. I was overwhelmed with waves of guilt about having left the Green Berets in my prime, knowing that Americans were still on the battlefield while I was wasting my skills, knowledge, and abilities—utterly useless and unoccupied—and found my way to the bottom of the bottle each night, spiraling further and further out of control. It is truly a tragic statistic that the generation of War on Terror veterans has now seen more suicides than killed-in-action, and the count continues to mount each year, long after the last boots stepped off the battlefield.

At the end of the day, it was a minor blip and speed bump in the grand scheme of things, but for an individual who'd spent his entire life attempting to define his identity through achievement, I was absolutely devastated and depressed, and the serendipitous timing set the stage for my physical and psychological availability for Evelyn Chang. The bottom line was that there was nobody I could talk to, nobody who understood how I felt, and nobody, it seemed, who cared enough to help me. I lashed out in every direction I could.

Unfortunately, I've since observed this phenomenon of self-immolation with more than a few transitioning veterans when we stumble, in different and varied forms, but the truth is that nobody owes us a damn thing because we all volunteered. The very nature of an owed transaction would negate the entire self-derived value of being a volunteer in the first place, and this is the essence of why the phrase "thank you for your service" is so cringeworthy and abhorrent to veterans—it debases one of the only pure things we privately savor from our sacrifices into a single, meaningless phrase—by making it seem as though some kind of social debt owed was satisfactorily paid up by uttering these magical words. I will always politely smile and say thank you back as I know it is well intentioned. But to say it makes us feel cheap is quite the understatement. Nevertheless, the real world built on numbers and logic dealt a humiliating lesson tattooed forever into my psyche when I found myself financially vulnerable and on the street for the first time in my life.

With no paycheck in sight and my savings tied up with my failing apparel venture, I bought time to figure out my next moves by couch surfing in a series of cramped Hong Kong apartments with my girlfriend, who had just left her cheerleading outfit company and was traveling with me, testing the limits of my friends' patience and generosity. It didn't take long for us to wear out our welcome.

Hero to zero in a flash. I had no idea where I was going to spend the night as I had been living out of a suitcase the past year undergoing a prolonged indoctrination for Palantir in its US offices, and all this occurred just as I was preparing to finally relocate to Singapore and find my own residence again. My girlfriend eventually bailed on me, flitting off to Cabo San Lucas to frolic with her friends at a bachelorette party. Honesty compels me to confess that a part of me was relieved. I might have been able to rebuild my life, or I might have been able to maintain my relationship with the princess, but I was not strong enough to do both.

Just when I thought things couldn't get any worse, somewhere, mentally buried deep in a pile of dirty clothes and shattered ambitions, my cell phone started to hum. I didn't even need to look. It was the only person in the world who ever called me unannounced. All I needed to do was close my eyes, and I could conjure her: my mother, her arms crossed, weariness and impatience and worry and, above all, disappointment inked in perfect calligraphy in her scowl. I was immobilized by the thought that I would have to share the news that I was on the unemployment line.

It may seem unbelievable that a man with my background and age would react this way to giving his mother a bit of bad news. But I'd be surprised if any of you who were not raised in a traditional Asian family could resist our parents' power and authority—never being good enough, no matter how many awards and accolades we bring back through the doors of our humble homes.

My mother is a true original, an inspiring and independent person in her own right. The youngest daughter of a venerable Kuomintang political family that fled from mainland China to Taiwan after the Maoist communist revolution in 1949, she is every inch an aristocrat, as much as she denies it. Her older brother became President of Taiwan. But though she tries mightily to hide it, there's also a rebellious streak in her. As a young woman, she immigrated to America, where she attended grad school and built a relationship with my father, despite the fact that her own father disapproved of him because my father's family was not as prestigious.

My mother treasures the ancient values that define—and frequently suffocate—Asian families. She was utterly selfless and endlessly devoted to us, but with my father at her side as the enforcer, a heavy hand with the leather strap and sometimes the back of his fist, my mother subconsciously tried to instill in us a desire to meet our obligations, not just to her but also to the entire universe of judgmental Asians. Study hard and get into a top university. Become a doctor or lawyer—more recently, a banker or engineer is acceptable too. Get a stable, high-paying job at a big-name company. Get married. Make sure your kids learn how to play piano and violin and how to speak Chinese. These obligations were hammered into us, both figuratively and, in my case, sometimes literally. My sister embraced them with grace and humility and joy. I was a bit less successful.

Looking back, I can see that I valued success as much as my mother did, but I defined it differently. I just wanted to be a badass mofo, whatever that was. But somewhere along the line, I had lost sight of that dream. Like many veterans struggling with the transition, I felt myself spiraling out of control with the sudden loss of task and purpose that had been so clearly issued and defined for me before.

I don't remember much about the phone conversation. My mother told me she was flying into Taipei to spend some time with my ailing grandmother, and she strongly suggested that I meet her there. I agreed. Filial duty aside, at least I'd have a roof over my head until I figured out my next steps. And then she made an offhand comment that caught my attention. The sister of an old school chum of my mother's—she had also gone to school with my uncle's wife, the first lady of Taiwan—had managed to get herself kidnapped while vacationing in the islands around eastern Malaysian Borneo, plucked straight out of her ocean villa in the dead of the night. My mother didn't know any of the details, or if she did, she didn't share them.

She didn't need to. I knew the place. I knew it as well as I knew the mean streets of Cupertino. I knew the kidnappers, or guys just like them at least. In fact, I had helped kill some of them. Even before I hung up, I already had a vague hunch that maybe, while I was killing time and looking for options in Taipei, I could be of some assistance. If I'd had any sense, at that moment, that Evelyn Chang's fate and my own would become linked, that once again, I was likely to take a crooked path forward, I kept it a secret from myself, and I certainly kept it a secret from my mother.

TAIPEI, TAIWAN

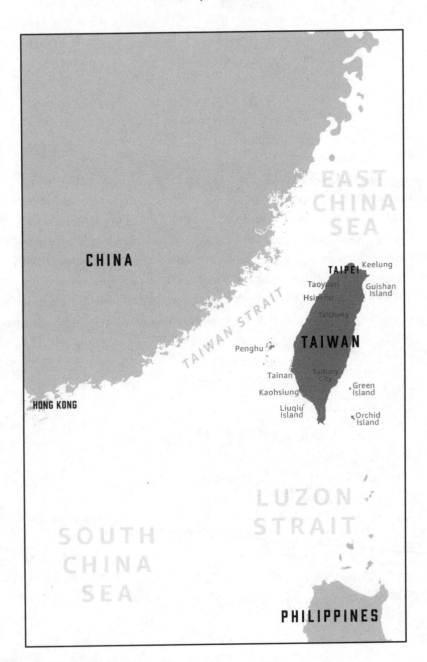

Chapter 8

Proof of Life

It was a homecoming of sorts for me, returning to Taipei to lick my wounds and maybe begin to find a way out of the hole I had dug for myself. I had always taken comfort in my grandmother's company, and in that place. It was a refuge for me, a time capsule of sorts, the epicenter of the motherland, you might say, as odd as that might sound, since I had not been raised there. Odder still when you consider that for my mother and her family, Taipei had never really been home. Home for the Ma family was on the mainland in Xiangtan, Hunan, where Mao Zedong was from, a place famous for spawning revolutionaries and rebels, and my family had been driven from there when the communists took over decades earlier. But they had carried the things that mattered with them when they fled, and in their mind, at least, the place had become a kind of shrine.

I felt a sense of relief—a feeling of peace almost—when I arrived at the eighteen-hundred-square-foot flat with its simple, dilapidated-style architecture of old Taiwan, its bare wood, its yellow tile floors scrubbed to a dull patina over the years. A vase of orchids sat by the door, surrounded by photos of my mother's family—my family. A portrait of my grandfather, formal and dignified, hung over the simple dining room table. And beside it, in my grandfather's meticulous, bold, and elegant calligraphy, were the family mottos: Books are treasures, gold is worth nil and All is hollow save works of goodwill (黃金非寶書為寶。萬事皆空善不空).

The very last words my grandfather ever said to me, shortly after I graduated from West Point and on a visit to Taipei, were that there was no greater honor or sacrifice in the world than serving as a military officer. It was important enough to him that he said it to me twice, stopping me on my way out the door to the airport. This shocked me, since I knew Chinese culture looked down on military service as work that only a mindless beast or a person whose only other option was prison would consider undertaking. He said these words to me as he pressed our family scrolls, written in his own hand, into mine. I looked up into his bright eyes for a moment and then he walked away, forever.

My family had always been guided by that principle. My mother, in her way, had been. Her older brother certainly had been. He had lived his entire life in service to his adopted homeland, first distinguishing himself as a Harvard Law School scholar and then in politics. He had risen to become the President of Taiwan, and yet despite that lofty position, he still made it a matter of principle to make his way each week to his mother's modest apartment for dinner. The paparazzi in Taiwan found ways to mock and criticize him for everything under the sun, including national news segments criticizing how his family briefly walked its new puppy off the sidewalk, but I always found his respectful devotion to my grandmother to be inspiring in a way, although it was not my way. Even with the burden of running a country, my uncle was still *xiaoshun*, or filial. He was a good son.

By the time I arrived in Taipei, though, the press had found a new issue to obsess about: the kidnapping of Evelyn Chang.

In many respects Taiwan is Asia's beloved little sister. It is genuinely rare to hear anyone speak ill of Taiwan, its people, or its culture in the region with anything but affection. Considered wealthy by the standard of emerging markets, but behind the power curve of the region's other three original Four Tigers and the behemoth of China, Taiwan is accustomed to allowing other more restive and aggressive countries to steal the international limelight while it gently goes about its own business, particularly in semiconductors and other high-precision manufacturing, where the little nation has gained global dominance. While Taiwan is forever exposed to potential aggressions by mainland China, there had never really been a sense that Taiwanese citizens needed to worry about a target on their backs, not at home, where many did not even bother to lock their doors, and not overseas. Evelyn Chang's kidnapping changed that in a heartbeat, and the press was in a frenzy.

In those first few days, virtually nothing was known about the details of the kidnapping or Evelyn's fate. No one even knew for sure whether she was dead or alive. Radio, television, and the front pages of every tabloid in the country were awash in wild speculation. Reporters—if you can call the ubiquitous paparazzi in the Taiwanese media "reporters"—had sussed out the bizarre six-degrees-of-separation link between Evelyn Chang and my uncle, a tenuous connection at best. The irony, of course, was that there ended up being a very direct connection between Evelyn and the President of Taiwan, which was when I naively wandered into the fray. Indeed, both my mother and my aunt, the President's wife and first lady of Taiwan, had attended the prestigious Taipei First Girls High School, with Evelyn's elder sister, Angela. That was no surprise: the Chang family had once been a fairly well-to-do Shanghai clan that, like my family, had fled to Taiwan after the communists won control on the mainland. But unlike most of the Kuomintang refugees in Taiwan, including my parents' families, the Changs had not fallen on hard times, and their early years in modern Taiwan were not marked by poverty. By the time of her kidnapping, Evelyn herself could be considered middle class, but she was far from a lady of leisure, and she was far, far removed from the circles of power in Taipei. She was a simple general manager at a small factory, a proverbial nobody who had been snatched almost at random.

The press could not imagine that—nobodies don't sell papers—and so in blaring coverage, Evelyn was depicted as a heartbeat away from the presidency, and her abduction, rather than being portrayed as a tragic but largely random crime, became a matter of national security, an international crisis of the highest order.

Opportunistic politicians would soon march to the beat of the tabloid drummers, demanding immediate and aggressive action to locate and free Evelyn Chang. If you turned on the TV anywhere in Taipei in those days, there was a good chance that it was focused on a backbencher from the Taiwanese government, demanding that the President *do* something. Precisely what that action might be, what it might achieve, whether it would have any chance of success, and why the nation's President should be personally involved, they had no idea. But that didn't stop them from braying.

The circus disgusted me. I had spent enough time undertaking delicate operations in dangerous corners of the world to know in my bones that if Evelyn Chang was alive, this kind of public hysteria would make matters worse for her. If she had, as some speculated, been kidnapped for ransom, the over-the-top antics of these lawmakers could only hurt her cause, convincing her kidnappers that they had indeed snatched a valuable victim. And when the kidnappers finally discovered—as they certainly would, sooner or later—that she wasn't vital to the Taiwanese national interest like the newspapers and politicians claimed, she would be in even greater peril.

My mother was disgusted too. When I arrived at my grandmother's flat, my mother was waiting for me. She had already compiled a list of potential Taiwanese employers who could throw a lifeline to her unemployed son, and driving me toward gainful employment was at the very top of her agenda. But she couldn't ignore the media din surrounding the kidnapping, and she couldn't turn her back on her lifelong friend Angela.

So she asked if I would join her the following morning at Yongkang Street, a popular street food alley in Taipei, where she was to meet with Angela. My mother didn't expect me to do much at the meeting. She knew very little about my military experience, the operations I had conducted, the peculiar skills I had developed over the years. That wasn't her fault. It's difficult to work such things into conversation over occasional family dinners or brief chats on the telephone. She did not expect—in fact she most assuredly did not want—that I would become actively involved. Instead, she wanted me to provide a sympathetic ear for an old friend, to offer comfort and reassurance where I could, and perhaps to help her friend brace herself for the tragedy that I suppose in my mother's mind was inevitable. Nothing else. She was adamant about that.

I have always felt a twinge of shame that I am not a deeply obedient and respectful son—not *xiaoshun* like my uncle. I took my own path, running off all over the world to follow wherever it led. But this time, perhaps because it was rare that I could ever help my mother with anything, I humbly and obediently agreed to the meeting.

Taipei was just waking as my mother and I made our way that morning, and the air in the market was perfumed with the scent of chicken stewing in soy and ginger. We grabbed a couple of pastel-colored stools, sat down at a simple stainless steel table, and waited for Angela. We didn't talk much. I watched people milling about the street while she absent-mindedly fiddled with a half dozen chopsticks arranged like pencils in a little plastic cup beside the paper napkins on the table.

My mother and I had expected a quiet meeting, just the two of us and Angela, but a few others from the extended Chang family surged in, four in all, led by Angela and her mother, an ancient woman, regal in a way but clearly in anguish, and Angela's daughter, Jennifer, an Asian American like me. Something about the way Angela looked at me was unsettling, a typical look of expectation mixed with skepticism that most aunties gave, a look that said, "All right, kid, show us what you've got." I was just a little Chinese boy to her, the son of her childhood friend.

As far as a I could tell, only one family member was missing: Richard Chang, the oldest brother and unlikely patriarch of the Chang clan. A ponytailed, sixtysomething biker who was always chasing younger women and faster motorcycles, wondering which one would kill him first, Richard had jetted off to Pom Pom Island as soon as the word got out about the kidnapping. He had intended to meet with the Malaysian authorities and—to the degree he could—try to collect information about the kidnappers. He also was there to handle repatriating the body of Eric Hsu on behalf of the Hsu family. In a black leather jacket and the fingerless gloves he wore even when he wasn't ripping up the streets of Taipei, Richard was the polar opposite of his stoic and matronly sister. But Richard also had a rare gift: a clear-eyed understanding of his own limitations, a kind of innate humility that he hid. It's a hard-earned lesson, knowing what you don't know, and a lot of soldiers and operatives never really master it. But Richard was self-aware enough to understand that he was in over his head, that the corrupt Malaysian authorities would, in all likelihood, be looking for a cut of whatever ransom might be paid and would perhaps even try to mislead him. So he let them try, and in the process, he had collected every bit of information they gave him, paying particular attention to what they let slip by accident, and then passed it all along to Angela and the family. Richard would continue to play that role, masterfully, throughout the case.

The picture he painted in those first desperate days was grim. There was little doubt in my mind that Evelyn had been taken by Abu Sayyaf. I could see in Angela's soulful, pleading, searching eyes that the terrorists had succeeded in at least one of their sadistic goals: to spread the pain of their crime as far as possible. Angela shared this pain with me. It came out, despite her stoicism and subtlety—it stirred something inside me. Like my mother, Angela had been forged by thousands of years of tradition. She was a strong and measured woman who succeeded in building the famous Regent Hotel in Taipei, and later had left Taiwan for America to find her own way. But this atrocity—the murder of her sister's common-law husband, the abduction of her sister, and the terrifying uncertainty over what would happen to Evelyn—was too much to bear alone. She looked to me for answers.

I conjured an image of Evelyn in captivity, though I now know that it was not nearly as horrific as the ordeal she was enduring. As we sat eating breakfast in that street market, Evelyn was suffering. In addition to going without her medicine for severe diabetes, the terror, the trauma, and the excruciating pain of a broken wrist that had gone largely untreated all worked together to break down this already-frail woman even further. With each passing day, it got worse, as if her own body was conspiring with her captors to find new ways to torture her.

And then there was the hunger. That word doesn't mean much to most people in the modern, market-driven first world. Even in the poorest pockets in America—in its most shameful inner-city projects and impoverished trailer park hollows—the poorest of the poor can usually find something to stave off that gnawing feeling in the pits of their stomachs. It may not be nutritious. It may not be enough to thrive. But it's enough, and that's true throughout the developed world.

True hunger, though, is a different creature altogether. It starts as discomfort, sure, but then it becomes real pain. Be it a trick of evolution, an act of mercy, or an act of sedition by a body against itself, that pain then subsides, and the body literally begins to consume itself. It dulls the senses, confuses the mind, and clouds a person's judgment. I have never experienced real hunger, but in my military training, I did come to the brink of it for prolonged periods of time that seemed never ending. I have seen hunger—even in a controlled environment like a US Army training program—weaken even the strongest men and turn members of the same unit against each other as it strips away all the niceties and reveals who you truly are in hard times. That's why it's part of the training. It's nothing special to be a good team player when you are warm, rested, and fed. It isn't lost on the Army that hunger can be a powerful adversary and that fatigue makes cowards of us all. Operating as a team through this mind-consuming hunger and stress in the wilderness for weeks on end is a highly effective tool to train soldiers to push beyond their limits, as will be required one day of them on the battlefield.

Evelyn Chang was hungry. Truly hungry. And her captors kept her that way. When they fed her at all, it was a bowl of thin gruel, barely enough to keep her alive, not nearly enough to keep her diabetes at bay. But that bowl of warm swamp water with a few grains of rice was enough to make her understand, even in her terror and confusion, that she was utterly dependent upon her captors.

Incredibly, in this environment, Evelyn again demonstrated an intuition for survival and deployed resistance techniques taught to future Green Berets at US Army Survival, Evasion, Resistance, and Escape (SERE) School to humanize herself to her captors. Weary of the verbal abuse, one day she pretended to be fascinated by their Islamic religious practices, and their demeanor toward her immediately changed. They were elated at the opportunity to convert her. She played along, sometimes sitting for hours and listening to them drone on, oftentimes not understanding what they were saying but always nodding and encouraging them. The rapport eventually led to Evelyn being able to speak freely and negotiate directly with the Abu Sayyaf leader numerous times as she attempted to engage in a battle of wits for her freedom and her life.

As a result of her efforts, once or twice, a couple of teenage boys in the camp, braving danger themselves, slipped Evelyn a warmed papaya to press on her injured arm. She'd accept it, pathetically grateful for that simple act of humanity. And then the abuse would resume.

Hunger and terror fogged her brain, and when the kidnappers demanded that she provide them with a telephone number for someone from whom they could demand her ransom, her mind went blank. She could remember only a single phone number, an old childhood boyfriend named Leo, a guy she hadn't spoken to in decades and had barely thought of since high school. And even that thought filled her with anguish, because she still did not know what had happened to Eric Hsu in the bloody chaos of the kidnapping.

Such is the way the mind works in extremis. Images of unimaginable terror collide at random with the mental equivalent of crumpled

Post-it Notes. Leo's was the only telephone number she could conjure. In fact, it wasn't even Leo's number. It was his mother's. Filial devotion is a common hallmark of all Asian cultures, and so while it may appear to some like the cosmic inertia of the universe aligned through a quantum loophole, or just an unbelievable stroke of luck, in Taiwan, it was perfectly normal that a middle-aged man like Leo had returned and was again living in his mother's house, caring for her in her elderly years.

And so the kidnappers called Leo's mother's house. It was an extraordinary act of serendipity that in the Philippines, where, at that time, even the most basic types of infrastructure like telephones often didn't work well, the call went through, and that Leo himself picked up on the second ring. The kidnappers allowed their injured, terrified captive to speak to a man she had not spoken to in many years and to pass along their demands.

That depraved display did have some value, I told Angela, as coolly and as confidently as I could. At least we knew for sure who was holding her, we had a sense of their demands, and, most importantly, for the first time since her abduction, we had proof of life.

There was now an open, albeit imperfect, line of communication. If nothing else, capable negotiators could use that to buy time, and maybe even find a way to spirit Evelyn's desperately needed diabetes medication to her.

Capable negotiators—there was the rub. I had spent enough time in this corner of the world, fighting Abu Sayyaf, to know that capable, honest, skilled, and experienced authorities were in short supply. The Philippines security landscape is extraordinarily complex and nuanced. The expensive but outstanding Lloyd's of London–affiliated kidnap-and-ransom consultants who called to pitch their services admitted they had never even been to the Philippines, which rendered them useless given my context of the challenging landscape. Evelyn's life hung by a thread, and the authorities in Malaysia would, I knew, make bold pronouncements about the case, but their tub-thumping was all for show, designed to appease the tourists of the resorts where kidnappings like this might occur, and then, hopefully, the story would be forgotten quickly. The local Malaysian authorities were always inclined to regard Abu Sayyaf carefully while also needing to watch their own backs, given the close historical ties of the Moro minority Muslim groups with their own people in the Malaysian state of Sabah, in Borneo (the Spanish referred to the Muslim peoples they encountered in the area as Moros, or Moors). As in any such case, corrupt local officials on both sides would also have plenty of opportunities to grease their own palms with a cut of any ransom that might be paid.

Things would not be much better on the Philippines side of the border. To be sure, there were capable, dedicated officials, military men guided by principles of honor and duty, and I had worked closely with many of them during my time there. But they had recently exhausted themselves in a pitched battle in the city of Zamboanga, fighting street by street, house by house, against those same terrorists. They had won the battle, but there was a sense of exhaustion from the seemingly never-ending problem in Mindanao.

For me, there was something else, something personal, about the Chang kidnapping.

It had been years since I had set foot in Zamboanga. I had first been sent there in 2006, as a kind of punishment, one last act of penance for the grave sin against military propriety that I had committed with the training / pizza party. My superiors saw it as a grave violation of the rules, grave enough to wash me out of the program with a NEVER TO RETURN stamp and a one-way ticket out of Fort Bragg. Then a chance encounter at a Seoul bookstore with rising 1st Special Forces Group Commander Rick Thomas years ago as a lieutenant while serving on the DMZ led to a new lease on life in the Green Berets. After I volunteered two weeks of holiday to work as a spare staff officer on a major exercise, he offered me a chance to serve for a year, basically as a US Army Special Forces intern, with a unique unit under his supervision that advised Korean special forces. After my expulsion from the Green

Beret training pipeline, Rick called the SERE School commander and told him that he did not care what Gene Yu did—he wanted him as a captain in his Group, pizza be damned, and suddenly I found myself reporting in the cold snow for a second winter SERE School visit. My military career had been salvaged, but since I was still somewhat on probation, I found myself effectively relegated to sitting behind a desk in the southern Philippines, about as far from the action as you could get in the Green Berets at the time.

That's not to say we didn't have any opportunities for action. We were responsible for the part of the global War on Terror playing out in Southeast Asia, and while most of the world's attention—and most of America's military resources—was focused on Afghanistan and Iraq, the region still had a great deal of turmoil and danger, particularly in the cauldron of violence and chaos in the jungles of the southern Philippines. In more ways than one, I found the mission required far more resourcefulness and creativity—which Green Berets are renowned for—in dealing with the complex low-intensity security environment of the Philippines when compared to my experiences in Kurdistan and Baghdad.

In hindsight, I'm pretty sure my bosses in Okinawa didn't think they were doing me any favors when they dispatched me to serve as a backup planning officer in a remote backwater called Camp Navarro, down in the main southern Philippine island of Mindanao, just outside the gritty city of Zamboanga.

It's misleading to call Navarro a camp. It was more like a prison yard that looked like a giant jungle gym, a tiny collection of rusting shipping containers set cheek by jowl in a tiny corner of a Philippine air force base, connected by a series of rusting steel-grate walkways connecting one container to the next above brownish, shin-deep water during the monsoons. Each container had been refitted to serve as a bedroom, with senior officers and enlisted lucky enough to have their own, while junior officers like me shared with two or three others. There was a depressingly small recreation area and tiny gym area that essentially was the center of our social lives. The whole place did not feel much bigger than the basketball gym in a typical American high school, and there was no escape from it.

We were, for all intents and purposes, prisoners in this sheet-metal gulag. Funny thing about the military: they prepare you for everything except the soul-crushing boredom and claustrophobia that are the real hallmarks of life in the Army.

The military had spent upward of a million dollars teaching me to kill, but they hadn't spent a dime teaching me how to kill time in a desolate place, and I was going stir crazy. There is a limit to the number of times you can play solitaire and sing karaoke oldies to nobody on the Magic Mike. So when my boss, a rising star Green Beret major named Scott Malone, recommended that I be tapped to help him plan an assault on a remote terrorist camp atop Mount Tumatangas—the Crying Mountain—I jumped at the chance.

At the beginning, our Filipino allies' top security threat was not the Abu Sayyaf terrorist group, and it was not the priority mission. It's not that they didn't appreciate the power of the American military, and it's not that they didn't value the hundreds of millions of American dollars that the United States was sinking into this struggle. Indeed, they valued that money a great deal. The influx of American training and resources over ten years undoubtedly elevated the quality of the Philippine military. It's just that they couldn't understand why we were so damned interested in what was essentially a gang of bandits who barely registered on Manila's radar, posses of shoeless pirates running wild in a place that most Filipinos, clustered closer to Manila, couldn't find on a paper map. As I've mentioned before, the Philippines is an incredibly difficult security environment, and it was not well known that eight of the nineteen hijackers who attacked the World Trade Center and the Pentagon on September 11, 2001, had connections to the southern Philippines.

To the Filipinos, Abu Sayyaf—this insignificant offshoot of Al-Qaeda—was simply not comparable to the existential danger that the regime faced from the world's longest-running communist insurgency, the New People's Army (NPA), which had been going on for decades. The Filipinos would indulge what they viewed as our bizarre obsession with these faraway and remote thugs, so long as we kept shoveling money into the region, money they could use to fight the communists and, in some cases, to feather their own nests. But they had no incentive to finish off Abu Sayyaf entirely. In the calculus of a country that had spent most of its history being exploited and devising devious ways to exploit their exploiters, that would have been like killing the goose that laid the golden hand grenade. While this was our impression as tactical operators at that time, the intense decade of real-world mission military exchange between the American and Filipino officers, soldiers, and units, have made the two organizations extraordinarily interlinked and interoperable today. It is no wonder, given how critically important this military alliance is for American security interests in Asia, not to mention the Philippines' geographical proximity to Taiwan.

Another factor complicated our objectives as well. Unlike the American military, which carefully cultivates a sense of loyalty to the Constitution first and consciously tries to prevent soldiers from developing attachments to a particular place, community, or even a particular unit, the Philippine military is very parochial. The soldiers who operate in a given region are often from that region, and in a place like Jolo Island, they are often connected—by culture, by experience, sometimes even by tribal and family ties—to the very people they are fighting. It's one thing to go to war against a stranger, but it's quite another thing to spill blood that possibly courses through your own veins as well. We tended to forget these sensitivities when we pushed for more aggressive action or pace of operations as foreigners.

Despite these structural and cultural challenges, the joint operation, with Filipinos on the front lines and US Army Special Forces advising from behind, had exacted a toll on Abu Sayyaf by the mid-2000s.

For example, the Green Berets had flooded the Basilan region with money through humanitarian aid events, even veterinarian events for farming animals like water buffalo, using it in an attempt help the Manila government buy the hearts and minds of the local populace. The Philippine military, sometimes reluctantly, drove the terrorists into an ever-shrinking area, where ultimately they were pushed out, soon fleeing to the main bastion of Jolo Island.

We were hoping to repeat that operation's success in the area around Mount Tumatangas, situated squarely on the western side of Jolo Island and its dominant terrain feature, except this time there would be nowhere (hopefully) for them to run. This was going to be a more complicated operation, simply because of the landscape and the culture. We would be trying to take the same ground from the same people who had bedeviled the famed general John. J. "Black Jack" Pershing a century and a quarter earlier, the same people who had been a thorn in imperial Japan's side during its World War II occupation. In the seventy-plus years since that era, nothing had changed except the names.

But we did have an advantage. The sheer laziness of our enemy would be our ace in the hole. Despite our success in Basilan, the terrorists at Mount Tumatangas did not seem particularly chastened. In fact, they didn't seem to be taking any special precautions in the aftermath of Basilan. For months on end, some forty of the organization's leaders huddled together in their mountain redoubt, at a place we called Camp Timahu. Later, while fighting insurgents in Iraq, I'd come to realize how utterly arrogant or incompetent that was. The leaders of the insurgency in Iraq would never have taken a risk like that, assembling their leadership in one place where they all could be taken out in a single operation. But experience had convinced the leaders of Abu Sayyaf that they had nothing to fear from the Philippine military or its American patrons. It galled me, I'll admit, to sit trapped in my glorified double-wide at Camp Navarro and watch, via our high-tech satellite surveillance systems, as the terrorist leader and forty of his henchmen almost frolicked in what to them—and to us at the time—seemed like a summer retreat.

I felt my irritation rising as I watched them go about their daily business, such as it was, seemingly without a care in the world. We had all the money we needed, all the high-tech toys to monitor them. We even had moles inside the camp. One was named Ramon. I was never particularly close to him, as he was being handled by CIA or other intelligence operatives in the camp on Jolo Island.

We gave Ramon a tracking device, inserted into his cell phone, and because he was the sort of person no one ever gave much thought to, he was able to sidle up to the powerful in the terrorist camp, including Khadaffy Janjalani, the Abu Sayyaf leader. Indeed, Ramon was often within arm's length of the commander, and so when he turned on the device to signal us, we knew generally where the leader was, even when he was out of sight of our eyes in the sky. That was invaluable intelligence, and it helped us shape the plan we would develop to take out not only the Abu Sayyaf leader but every one of his forty top lieutenants.

The plan we developed was as old as the art of war, effectively a hammer-and-anvil tactic. With the terrorists gathered in their camp, we'd launch an offensive, with the Filipino soldiers and marines doing the bulk of the fighting while, in keeping with the demands of Filipino politicians, US Army Special Forces ODA teams would observe and guide from behind the lines.

That, too, frustrated me but was way above my pay grade. Maybe it was the fact that I was a twentysomething hotshot who, unlike many of my classmates at West Point, had not yet gotten a chance to prove my chops in battle. I'd get a chance later, in other places, to be the first one to kick down the door, and I'd do it often enough that it lost its luster. But at that moment I was supposed to be in the background, so I tried to be a good soldier and do what I had been told.

It took my planning boss—the major—and me about a month to plan the operation, and I quickly discovered not only that I had a knack for outlining tactical operations, but also that I enjoyed it. The geeky kid from Cupertino relished the intricate details, and I took great pride in producing elaborate PowerPoint presentations for the brass, which the American and Filipino officers alike always greeted with admiring comments. Being good with PowerPoint was openly ridiculed in the military, but I needed any pat on the back I could get after the pizza incident.

I had dutifully sought their input and had gotten some valuable insights, particularly from the US Navy and Air Force officers attached, for helping me plan Filipino naval asset and airstrike support, but an operation like this depended on a major amphibious assault. Probably only the US Marines had the necessary expertise, although not from actual combat since we were pretty sure nothing like this size of an amphibious infantry raid operation had been conducted recently, and those we had in our headquarters were not infantrymen. So with only three Green Berets at Navarro, one being the commander, we did our best research, poring through US Marine Corps manuals on amphibious assault operations, and we wrote the whole damn thing ourselves and gave it to our counterpart Filipino generals.

When the time came to turn the plan into action, I boarded a helicopter and headed to Jolo Island to brief the ODA teams attached to Philippine infantry battalions and other special operations units and prepare for the attack on the ground as a temporary battle captain, or a coordinating officer, in the headquarters at Camp Bautista next to Jolo Town, the capital. Soon, the Green Beret company deployed to Jolo from Okinawa dragooned me into the battle captain position permanently from Zamboanga, quickly realizing I wasn't just a useless pizza boy. I spent the next several months sharing a dilapidated large barracks room with twenty other protein-shake-eating Green Berets and its various headquarter staff with open-air public latrines and no air-conditioning in the humid and steaming jungle. It was an oddly peaceful and quiet life during these days, waking every morning to the sound of the roosters calling in the day. Then word came down from Manila that the politicians and the diplomats—the old men who really run every war, and have since the beginning of time—had given us the green light.

We were confident in our plan. It was simple. It was elegant. Six hours before dawn, a contingent of a few hundred Philippine marines and a newly formed Light Reaction Battalion (the Philippine equivalent of ████████████████████████████████████ ███ would land on the beach, cut about three kilometers through the jungle, and head up the mountain. Just before they hit the camp, I'd help coordinate with the beloved and respected Filipino marine general, the great Juancho Sabban, to push a button from his post on Jolo, raining hell down on the terrorists with artillery fire, and when they fled downhill, as they surely would, they'd run right into the anvil: several battalions of Philippine infantry, thousands of soldiers, all individually advised by one of our very capable A Teams. It was an enormous operation, and I felt like I was part of history just being there.

It was practically foolproof. Or so we thought.

They say that no battle plan survives first contact with the enemy. On Jolo Island, it barely survived first contact with the soldiers executing it. A key component of the plan was fundamentally counter to their jungle warfare doctrine of avoiding movement in the night. I had arrogantly assumed that the Philippine forces we deployed by sea wouldn't have the skills to cut through the jungle and launch their assault with anything like the speed or alacrity of US Army Special Forces. We're trained to find our targets and neutralize them before they even know what's hit them, and our teams are filled with America's best physical specimens. I figured the Philippine special forces would at least be the equivalent of our everyday American infantry units and their official standards for speed of movement, so we allotted three hours for them to cross a few klicks of jungle, which I thought would be plenty to spare.

I was too inexperienced with working with Asians to know that they would never admit they could not keep up with American standards as a matter of face and honor. I did not yet understand that this Asian value not only allows for dishonesty in these situations but even expects it. I also did not know that as a matter of doctrine, they rarely fight in darkness, to include movement, and it is nearly impossible for a large group in jungle mountain terrain to navigate and stay quiet, even with advanced night vision. This is why the Scout Rangers usually move in small seven-man teams. And so as soon as they landed, the plan started to unravel. They dawdled and wandered, and seven hours after the first inflatables had bumped up against the beach, they still hadn't made it up the mountain, now glowing in the pale-blue light of morning.

At the time, as there were no Green Berets allowed to move that close to the front lines with the assault elements, and communications apparently were not working on the Filipino side, I could not tell you whether it was run-of-the-mill incompetence or something more nefarious that cost us the cover of darkness and the element of surprise. I know now that I should have simply checked with the real troops on the ground and adjusted the timeline accordingly. This basic error led to creating an entire plan around a main effort action that was never possible to follow in the first place. It is incredible to reflect that I alone was left with this planning detail and my oversight on confirming a reasonable timeline contributed to a glaring failure of this large-scale operation.

Within minutes of the botched landing, the point of the spear was blunted, if not broken altogether. As the sun began to break the horizon, threatening to expose our operation, I realized that the whole plan was in jeopardy.

We had no choice at that point, so even though the assault team was still too far from the mountaintop to be of any use at all, I muttered a few curses, requested permission by radio with my Green Beret colonel back in Zamboanga, and ran down to General Sabban's headquarters. I convinced him to order the artillery barrage. From my observation post miles away, at the top of the water tower at Camp Bautista, even in the stark light of morning, I could see the mountain light up like the Fourth of July and feel the ground beneath me trembling. I was twenty-six years old.

Push the button. From five miles away. It sounds so distant, so detached, so technical and antiseptic. "Joystick combat," some call it. A great many people will tell you that America's technological supremacy has turned combat, for US soldiers at least, into a kind of deadly computer game, impersonal and cold, war by remote control, drained of what little humanity there ever was in combat.

Those people don't know what the hell they're talking about.

For centuries, ever since the invention of the longbow, war has almost always been at arm's length. In World War II, the enemy was little more than a gray silhouette in a winter fog, viewed through the sights of an M1 Garand from a quarter mile away. These days, our billion-dollar eyes in the skies bring us up close and personal with our enemies. Our surveillance of the Abu Sayyaf camp was so specific, so intricate, that we could sit at the computer screen in the Sensitive Compartmented Intelligence Facility (SCIF) and practically count the hairs on the chins of the young terrorists. For hours on end in the days leading up to the attack, we were like ghosts stalking the camp, utterly unseen, and because we were invisible, we got to see what each individual person was like when his guard was down. These weren't anonymous silhouettes in the fog. We had come to know these one hundred people, if only by their quirks and idiosyncrasies—when the time came to push the button, we knew something specific, something unique, about every man we helped kill.

In the smoke and chaos, I could not see them die. We'd later learn that the barrage had achieved at least one of our objectives: it had seriously wounded Khadaffy Janjalani, the Abu Sayyaf leader at the top of the list of terrorists we had been hoping to take out. The survivors carried his mangled body through the jungle, and as I sat there at my post, I could watch their progress as they stumbled and fled. Unexpectedly, Ramon, our mole, was right there at Janjalani's side, despite having been warned to stay away for a period of seven days. A little purple dot on my screen from the signal we had planted in his phone betrayed their every move.

The fleeing terrorists stopped to catch their breath on a mountain path, out of reach of the soldiers that formed the anvil but not out of range for me and the artillery we oversaw. I ran down again to the white house and requested a second strike. "I advise to use all remaining munitions," I said. The good general agreed, and it was every bit as devastating as the first strike, with hundreds of rounds of 105-millimeter explosive High-Explosive Anti-Tank (HEAT) shells, each capable of vaporizing anything within twenty yards. By the time the smoke cleared, we had killed about a third of the hundred or so terrorists.

Janjalani, however, had escaped death. That time. Months later, during follow-on assaults, Janjalani would indeed be killed in a confrontation with a company of Philippine Scout Rangers. But despite the fact that Janjalani had temporarily cheated death, the body count that day was enough for the careerists in the US Army to declare the operation a success. To this day, when the Philippine military talks about what came to be known as Operation Ultimatum, they speak of it in deferential tones, as if recounting a great victory, as it did serve as the model for follow-on Ultimatum campaigns for years, which met much higher degrees of success. Today, the entirety of the repeated efforts against Abu Sayyaf around Mount Tumatangas are referred collectively as Operation Ultimatum.

In my eyes, at that time believing we had only one shot, Operation Ultimatum was a colossal failure. I also observed a second attempt two years later in 2008, which was unimaginatively named Operation Ultimatum II, where the Abu Sayyaf leadership shockingly went right back to Camp Timahu for the summer retreat again. This time I was much more on the sidelines, but I found myself again at Camp Bautista for about a month leading a joint counterterrorist team of Green Berets and Navy SEALs advising the Joint Special Operations Group, the Philippines equivalent of ███████████████████████████ ████████████████████████████, led by the intrepid colonel Ramon Dizon. The mission had a nearly identical plan and outcome. I frustratedly wondered why nobody had come to ask my opinion before they dusted off the earlier plan that failed, the one where I had repeatedly elaborated the need to plan the operation to be executed during daylight hours in a lengthy report. The US Army is incredibly efficient in some areas but appallingly horrible at business continuity planning and operations by private-sector standards.

I would later be haunted by several men we didn't kill at both ironically named Ultimatums. We left many alive, but three key Abu Sayyaf lieutenants in particular survived. Yasser Igasan, Idang Susukan, and Sihata Latip were still operating with near impunity in the jungles of Jolo, overseeing atrocities and engineering the kidnapping of vulnerable foreigners, including Evelyn Chang. I didn't tell the Changs any of this over breakfast, but Evelyn's kidnapping was, for me, somewhat personal.

I directed all the frustration of that time in my life at Abu Sayyaf for daring to bring our little game across the line and into my personal life. I wasn't making it in the real world, but maybe if I could help here, it would remind me that I still had something of value to offer. Evelyn Chang was a friend of our family, of my mother, and I felt compelled to at least make a few phone calls, maybe take a few meetings in Manila, perhaps point the right people in the right direction. My whole life has been a story of second shots, and maybe, I thought, I could be a little bit *xiaoshun*, just this once.

Officially, Taiwan could do next to nothing. Despite Taiwan being the continuous legitimate government of the Republic of China since 1911, the Chinese Communist Party has convinced the world to limit diplomatic ties with a vibrant, full-fledged democratic country that continues to operate peacefully, with its own central bank–controlled currency, its own military, its own political system, its own society. The Republic of China has never been fully conquered (nor has it surrendered) and thus has always existed since its founding in 1911; it has functioned as an entirely independent country for the last seventy years, contained to the island of Taiwan and a smattering of outlying islands, and as a full democracy since 1990.

These politics matter to this story because Taiwan does not have formal diplomatic, military, or law enforcement relations with the Philippines, thus handicapping the Taiwanese authorities' ability to reach into multiple levels of peer-to-peer security relationships formed over years or even decades of engagement. The Taiwanese government couldn't exert official influence or assemble a credible joint effort with Taiwanese resources, support, and oversight. So hardly anything was being done on the Philippine side, and without political leverage or existing relationships, nothing *could be* done from the Taiwanese side. At least nothing quickly enough to save Evelyn Chang's life before Abu Sayyaf grew discouraged at securing a sizable ransom and decided to use her beheading as a new propaganda video.

So effectively, nobody else was helping the Chang family. The Taiwanese government was hobbled by its parochial and dogmatic adherence to process and rules, which limited it to dealing with Interpol, which in turn had only been able to secure a single lowly buck sergeant from the Philippine National Police as a point of contact to the Chang family at that time. As absurd as it seemed, I realized that I might be the best credible resource to help engineer Evelyn's release, if I got lucky with a few phone calls.

From another perspective, I also saw it as a continuation of the Green Beret conflict with Abu Sayyaf, a conflict that I knew and understood, and I was entirely available for the first time in my life.

I said none of this aloud during that morning's breakfast. Instead, as my mother and I left the table, I made a few bland and noncommittal promises to reach out to some people I knew in the US and Philippine militaries to see what I could find out. The Chang family's eyes were all on us as we left.

Once we were out of earshot, my mother squeezed my arm. "You'd better not be thinking about helping them or doing anything crazy," she said.

I forced a laugh, as if to say, *I wouldn't even consider it.*

But in my mind, I was already on a plane for the Philippines. I did not think twice about sacrificing the thousands of dollars I had already paid six months ago for a climbing trip to the base camp of Mount Everest in Nepal with my closest Hong Kong friends. This was a crisis, one that was directly affecting friends of my family. It was fraught with danger, yes, but also rich with purpose, not least the purpose of helping a vulnerable woman and her distraught family. All my problems suddenly seemed small in comparison and I found sanctuary in focusing on Evelyn's crisis instead of mine. I felt the pull of a simple calling, a chance to achieve a clear mission and objective again. I couldn't then see all the factors that had conspired to drive me back to the Philippines, but I knew for certain I had unfinished business there in more ways than one.

PHILIPPINES

Chapter 9

With Friends like These

I thought about firing the Viking on the spot.

Those icy-blue Nordic eyes narrowed as he stared off into the distance, far beyond the pulsing pink lights of the go-go bar in Manila's famed red-light district on Burgos Street, past the bar girls and the half dozen bottles of watered-down, price-jacked booze that littered our table, as if focusing on some distant, imaginary Valhalla.

"Seriously?" I asked him. "You believe in all those Viking gods? Like Thor and stuff?"

He grabbed the table with a pair of arms like pale-white pythons, pushed back in his chair, and tried to stare me down. "That's comic book shit," he said in an Icelandic accent at once both menacing and lilting. "I'm talking about the old gods, the ones in charge in olden times when guys like you and me, we could kill each other on the battlefield, and then drink together, take women together, and meet later that same night in Valhalla, covered in glory."

That was not the last time he'd invoke the image of mortal combat with me. Indeed, later on in our relationship, he once threatened to pick me up and hurl me thirty-eight floors from the balcony of a Manila building. But at that moment, in the pink haze of the girly bar, I was not quite sure whether he was being serious, and so, as I would later do on that balcony, I played it cool.

I did my level best to keep a poker face, but I must have been signaling something because his twitchy sidekick, a shapeless middle-aged Filipino with a killer's lifeless eyes and a fishing vest bristling with weapons, shot me a look that was half warning, half threat.

You could have cut the tension with a machete. But just then a bar girl, too young to drink in America but old enough to work the foreigners in this place, sidled past our table, and the Viking, as I preferred to call him, slapped her ass and let out a lewd guffaw. She responded with a well-rehearsed girlish giggle. She didn't seem offended, and I chalked it up to the kind of boorish behavior you expect in a joint like this.

I'll confess that it was not my first rodeo. The two oldest professions in the world are prostitution and soldiering, and in my experience, they go hand in hand. Hell, when the ancient sages wrote the sagas that so influenced the Viking, that was exactly what they were talking about. Fight all day, fuck all night, forever. Okay, so this bar at the flickering end of Manila's red-light district may not have been Valhalla, but it was one of thousands of places in every seedy corner of the world where soldiers and soldiers of fortune establish their bona fides and build rapport and trust over booze and lechery.

"You know I saw you before, in Baghdad, when I was with Blackwater," he said, suddenly jovial. "At the airport, ██████████████. You sort of stood out. There weren't a lot of Asian special forces officers—or any type, come to think of it—coming through there."

"I think I would have remembered you," I said, scanning the faces I could recall from my prolonged stay at ███████████████████ ████████████████████ of the Baghdad International Airport, back when I was leading a counterterrorist ODA team and fighting side by side with the Iraqi national mission force, the most elite crisis response unit in the country.

"Maybe I didn't want you to remember me," he said.

I thought, *What the hell have I gotten myself into?*

The Viking told a lot of stories, some of them true, but little was known about his actual background. He had, it was said, slipped out of Iceland almost twenty years earlier, one step ahead of the law, although what he did to upset the authorities in his homeland remained clouded in myth and speculation. In the years since, he had worked as a private military contractor, the current euphemism for a mercenary, a role that has been an integral part of combat for thousands of years. The Viking's job in Iraq had been to weld reinforced armor onto our vehicles and repair Humvees damaged by improvised explosive devices (IEDs), and in that post, like most contractors, he had often found himself spelunking through the black market and rubbing shoulders with the less savory characters who always seem to gravitate toward the edges of any large-scale military operation.

In time the Viking had come to think of himself as kind of a swashbuckling pirate type. True to his heritage, he had salt seas in his blood. He was an extremely experienced boat captain, having been accredited by the Lloyd's of London insurance market as a superyacht captain. He told me that he'd once actually built a Viking longboat, the type of vessel that his forebears had used to terrorize Europe a millennium and a half ago, and that he'd actually sailed it—alone and crewless—to the coast of France to simulate and harness the spirit of his marauding ancestors. I never said this to him, but I always supposed that it was a good thing he had not been able to find a crew. What might have happened to those pristine little towns clinging to the coast of France with a bit of drink in a group of Vikings? His crooked career path had taken him from Iceland, through Iraq, across Asia, and finally to the Philippines, where he dabbled in everything but made most of his money as a smuggler.

"Anything except women, children, and drugs," he said, describing his business plan.

Concise, I thought. It could fit on a business card.

I had never even heard of the guy until a few days earlier. As I had promised Angela and Jennifer in the hours after our breakfast meeting,

I sifted through my list of old contacts to see if I could find anyone who might be of assistance. But it had been several years since I had left the military, and I had worked diligently to remake myself into anything other than a soldier, still salty over the nature of my departure. Besides, it had been a hell of a lot longer than that since I had last set foot in the Philippines, though not much had changed there since my last tour of duty. Hell, not much had changed there in the last three hundred years, particularly in the provinces outside Manila.

The ancient religious, political, and tribal blood feuds marched on, as bloody as ever, and corrupt and incompetent authorities still schemed to figure out how they could turn conflict into a payday in the reverberating mess left by colonial imperialist powers. As with so many similar places in the world, nothing had changed but the faces. Most of the senior Filipino and American special forces guys I knew had moved on. And to those who remained, well, I was a civilian now; they had no reason to talk to me.

In my mind, I was still a Green Beret. I always would be—whether or not I still wore the green beanie or strapped myself with long and short guns on the daily. I did not need a piece of paper or a uniform to keep what the training and combat had instilled in me: the skills, the knowledge, the capabilities. But in the eyes of my old contacts, I was now just some moneygrubbing civilian. One or two of the American guys I used to know—from my leadership team at Palantir, former Okinawa-based US Army Special Forces and US Navy intelligence guys—had been sympathetic enough to throw me a crumb. They checked the phone number through their contacts with American intelligence assets in the area and confirmed for me that Evelyn was indeed on Jolo Island, and near Maimbung, where my former team, ODA 121, had served during Operation Ultimatum before I joined them. It wasn't much. But it was something.

Apart from that, though, every phone call I made was a dead end. It was only as a last resort that I'd reached out to Matt Pecot, my old boss, a great friend and even greater mentor at Credit Suisse, the guy who had pulled me into the world of high finance from the Green Beret fraternity. He still had enough connections to the old world that he knew a ███ guy who knew a guy. And that was how I came to meet the Viking.

He wasn't easy to get in touch with. When I finally reached him, I persuaded myself that maybe, just maybe, this loose cannon had the connections I needed. After our first telephone conversation, I grew a little more confident in his abilities and in his network of operatives in the Philippines, most of them criminals themselves. I also realized immediately that there was no way this Odin-worshipping pirate and Angela, the prim, reserved woman who was acting—with her mother's blessing—as the voice of the Chang clan, would be able to work together without a go-between. I had deluded myself when I thought I could simply vet the Viking and his team, pass them off to Angela, and then get back to the task of figuring out what to do with my life. There was no one else—in Taiwan or the Philippines or anywhere else in the world—who could navigate those two utterly different worlds, not to mention the language barrier. And I would not be able to do it from a safe distance.

And so, a day or so after our breakfast meeting, I had requested that Angela withdraw $20,000 in US currency from the family's account. I would use just a tiny bit of it to outfit myself for a very brief trip to the Philippines. This was for expenses only, I told her. I couldn't think of any honorable way to take payment for the work, not from people who were in such need and distress. The Viking was a different matter, of course, and the majority of that $20,000 would go straight to him and his team, a retainer for ten days of work. I'd later learn that it was not an exorbitant fee for such a dangerous service as high-risk crisis consulting. Still, the money made Angela blanch. She came up with it, but what really alarmed her was what was drawing me ever more deeply into the case. She was aghast at the idea. She knew my mother well enough to know that she would be beyond outraged to learn that I was involved in this morass, and that she would blame Angela for manipulating me.

To be honest, I had pretty much the same fear. We'd keep this between ourselves, I told Angela, and if all went well, then I'd be back in a day or two, after checking out the Viking and making sure everything was good to go, before my mother even knew I was not in Hong Kong, which is what I had told all my Taiwan connections, or Taipei, as I had told all my Hong Kong connections.

I used my own money to buy a few things that I didn't mind picking up anyway. It had been a while since I had maintained what my training and experience had taught me to call a "go-to-hell bag," filled with all the things I'd need in case I had to pop smoke at the drop of a hat for some real or imagined wrong I had done somebody, so I gathered a compass, a decent pair of boots, some cargo pants, and a good folding knife—basic survival gear. Hope for the best. Plan for the worst.

And then, with Angela's reluctant blessing and my mother kept in blissful ignorance, I quietly hopped aboard a plane, and the next thing I knew, I was in Manila.

It had been at least five years, and I felt a little less certain of myself this time around. During my last trip through this airport, I was wearing the uniform of the United States Army (figuratively, since special forces operators never travel in uniform). I had come to think of it as a kind of shield, a camo-colored calling card that told anybody who saw me not to mess with me because I had the world's biggest gangster backing me up. This time, I was just some guy, a goofy foreigner with a carry-on bag, a potential mark for any con, a target for any predator. But I was also representing a potentially lucrative ransom payment, to whoever knew I was representing the Chang family or that I was the nephew of the sitting President of Taiwan, and that made me a valuable target too—especially in a place like the Philippines where a dollar means a lot more to them than it does to you and me. It made me uneasy. For the first time since I had left the Army, I missed the uniform and the protection it afforded me. I also missed the access it had granted me to trustworthy American operators. Now that I was a civilian, they no longer wanted or needed to help me. On the contrary, most of them wanted to stay as far from the Evelyn Chang matter as possible. To them, I was a risk to their career security. Having come from that world, I don't blame them, though I don't apologize for asking for their help. But it drove home for me that I was very much on my own. Whatever happened, there would be no AC-130 gunship to call as was the case in Iraq, and no ███████████ was coming to save me, or to recover my body and return it with a folded flag to my mother. It was just me, the Viking, and whatever freelance psychopaths he happened to have in his employ at that moment.

The Viking had arranged to have one of his Philippines intelligence agency contacts meet me and escort me quickly through the immigration line, in order to stay less visible at customs. The associate quickly whisked me out of the airport, into a car, and on toward the luxurious digs that the Viking had reserved for me—under an assumed name, of course—at the famed Peninsula Hotel, where General Douglas MacArthur used to hold court when he ruled the Philippines, back in the days when America called the country its colony.

In any other corner of the world, the Peninsula would have been a five-star hotel, but it had lost a little bit of its luster five years earlier, when the lobby had been riddled with gunfire during a pitched battle between the supporters of an insurgent senator, Antonio Trillanes IV, and then Vice President Teofisto Guingona Jr. By the time I checked in, of course, you could barely tell that an armored personnel carrier had once burst through the glass doors that I now sauntered through.

In a way, I thought, the Peninsula was emblematic of the Philippines, a place where all the strands of this country's complex history were rendered in architectural detail, with influences drawn from all the countries that had tried to control it, but if you looked closely, you could see the plaster patches where the bullets had hit and get a sense of the seething chaos beneath the surface.

I had studied that chaos when I was first deployed to the Philippines, and I had gotten very familiar with the history of it all. I knew that the Spanish had tried, with all their wealth and all their might, to subdue the restive populace, and that they had failed. I knew the story of how the United States had also been thwarted, how "Black Jack" Pershing had met his match among the Moro, the great-great-grandfathers of the same terrorists who now held Evelyn Chang. These were wild, fearsome fighters who had turned a crude machete—a weapon called a bolo—into an instrument of pure terror. The Americans had learned the hard way that these killers were too mean to die, that you could pump any number of rounds into them and they'd still keep coming. Indeed, that's why the Americans invented the famed Colt 1911, a .45 semiautomatic pistol that became the sidearm of choice for American military officers for a hundred years, a weapon designed specifically to knock a raging Moro off his feet. And even that wasn't enough to subdue the Moro. They called themselves something different now, but they were the same enemy the Spanish had fought, the same enemy General Pershing had fought, the same enemy that, as a military observer, I had watched decimate a Filipino Navy SEAL detachment that tried to land on a remote beach. I could still see the panicked operators on my intel feed, their weapons waterlogged and useless: the men bogged down in chest-deep water, the few who made it to the beach, and those who dove for cover and swam back to their watercraft to escape the relentless machine-gun fire from the Abu Sayyaf terrorists on the beach.

After settling into my hotel room, the Viking and his snarling cur of a sidekick, Roland, squired me out for a steak dinner—rare, of course—and thence to Plan-B, the go-go bar where, naturally, the Viking was a part owner. The girls who worked there treated him like a king, and between shots of cheap booze, which give much worse hangovers than real whiskey, the Viking gave me a rundown on the status of Abu Sayyaf.

When I was last in the Philippines in 2008, the terrorist group had been reduced to maybe thirteen hundred fighters. I was a key campaign planner and battle captain in taking out about forty high-value targets in the first phase of Operation Ultimatum. But despite the government's effort to contain the group and American officers claiming the success of the effort over the years, I discovered Abu Sayyaf had in fact grown in the years I had been gone, and the group was in many ways more dangerous than ever. That which does not kill you makes you stronger, the old saying goes, and this latest iteration of the war against the modern Moro, with the "soft power" of the United States standing meekly behind the Philippine military, had certainly not killed off Abu Sayyaf or any of the other myriad groups who, in the chaos and confusion of the Philippines, continued to fight, sometimes with each other, sometimes against each other, sometimes as a bloc, and sometimes as renegade units. These armies of shifting allegiances had not been neutralized, neither as a threat nor as a movement. Even Mother Nature seemed to have conspired to steel the terrorists. A vicious typhoon had recently ripped through the region and actually been a boon to the terrorists. Not only had its damage added an additional layer of chaos, in which groups like Abu Sayyaf flourish, but it had also boosted the group's standing in the eyes of the local people. The ineffectual government in Manila had not been able to get food, water, or medical supplies to the ravaged people of the region, but Abu Sayyaf could. The group had gained stature among the people while the government lost face, hearts, and minds. When people who have next to nothing lose it all, when they have nothing left to lose, glorified street gangs like Abu Sayyaf find themselves swarmed with new recruits. I had seen the same thing happen in Iraq, I had seen it in Kurdistan, and now, the Viking told me, it was happening here, again.

Know your enemy, Sun Tzu said. That's a lesson that's drilled into American military officers from the first time they pin on their bars. It's harder than it sounds. To know your enemy, you first have to know yourself, and to understand that if you had nothing and lost even that, then you, too, might find yourself seduced by the promises made by groups like Abu Sayyaf when that promise comes with a bowl of broth and a sense of an identity and place in the world. A warrior ultimately has little control over which team they were born to join.

I was pretty sure I knew my enemy. I wasn't quite as sure that I knew my friends. Despite his Nordic flamboyance, despite his over-the-top mercenary braggadocio, there seemed to be a kind of earnestness to the Viking. He was in his element in the Philippines. Like a lot of these guys, he had a checkered past and was very much at home among a swamp of corruption, but he also seemed to have a twisted sense of honor, and I eventually respected him as both a partner and a friend. I can't say the same of his sidekick, Roland. Something about the way that shapeless mole of a man looked at me, always out of the corner of his eye, put me on edge. I could feel anger and resentment in the guy's twitchiness, and I got the feeling that, in a place where US$100 could hire a killer for a drive-by on his moped, Roland was the kind of guy to offer you a low rate and then cut your throat when you paid him. And just in case I had any doubts, Roland proved it. At one point during the strip club summit, when the Viking excused himself from the table to slap a few more asses, Roland opened his fishing vest to show me the arsenal he had hidden inside: a couple of handguns, a few magazines, a seriously menacing knife, and two ankle-holstered snub-nosed pistols. That was the closest I ever came to seeing him smile.

It's not that Roland, if that was his real name, didn't have a few bona fides himself. Before he was the Viking's sidekick, Roland had what passes for a fairly successful career in intelligence. He had allegedly been a subregional head of the National Intelligence Coordinating Agency (NICA), the Philippines' shadowy, ethically challenged version of the CIA by reputation, in one of the regionalities in Mindanao, an organization known to use assassination almost as a matter of routine, though they never confirmed it. Prior to meeting Roland, I had never encountered any NICA operative before. Looking at him, though, I could see how he might have risen to the top of that particular organization, although later through my trusted NICA operatives, we were unable to confirm his identity.

"You go to war with the army you have, not the army you wish you had," Donald Rumsfeld once famously said. Sitting there in that girly bar, I realized that this was the army I had. So be it. We play the cards we are dealt.

Roland reined in his menace when the Viking returned, nodding obsequiously as the Viking briefed me on what he had done so far. He had a few operatives in the Jolo region, he said, ghosts on mopeds and small motorcycles who could flit through the villages and byways and had collected a little bit of valuable intelligence. They had confirmed that Evelyn Chang had been sighted in the Maimbung area, and that she was in the hands of a comparatively small group of terrorists. The intelligence confirmed what I had been able to glean from the American military and Palantir guys I had spoken to the night before. There was some seriously bad news too. Remote as their ramshackle camp was, the kidnappers still had cell phones. They had gotten wind of the media frenzy in Taipei and were thoroughly convinced that they had snatched a valuable prize, that Allah had gifted them a hostage whose ransom would make them all rich.

I don't know if the Viking believed me when I told him that Evelyn's family did not have the kind of money that the terrorists were likely to demand. Judging from the look in Roland's beady little eyes, I was pretty sure he didn't believe me at all.

But the Viking had an idea. There was a woman Roland knew, a kind of imperious local warlord who had the respect of the terrorists— she called them "my boys"—and the status and standing to negotiate with them directly.

She called herself Lady Ann, and the Viking proudly informed me that she would deign to meet with me. In fact, Roland had already taken the liberty of arranging the meeting.

It sounded like a promising starting point, and I agreed. That night, as I lay tossing and turning in the giant, sumptuous bed in my suite at the Peninsula Hotel, it started to dawn on me that it was likely going to take more than a day or two to navigate all the corrupt crosswinds in this case. I could probably handle Lady Ann, I thought to myself, and I was sure I could work with the Viking. Roland was a wild card, and dangerous. Soon I would learn just how dangerous he could be.

BAGHDAD, IRAQ

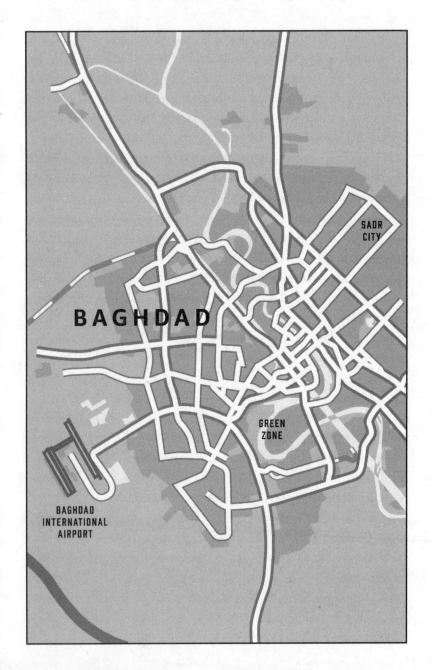

Chapter 10

Operation Amir

There was something else I hadn't told the Chang family, or my mother, or the Viking, something I barely acknowledged even to myself in those immediate chaotic days after Evelyn's kidnapping. I knew they were all looking to me as the voice of calm professionalism, the expert in dealing with savage terrorists and kidnappers. And, yes, I was indeed quite familiar with Yasser Igasan, who was a sort of spiritual leader of Abu Sayyaf, and the other two key operational lieutenants, Idang Susukan and Sihata Latip, who had also escaped death in Operation Ultimatum. I understood his followers as well as I understood him. I knew their tactics, and I had seen the brutality they were capable of inflicting on the innocent. I understood their almost-adolescent rage, and I recognized their weaknesses.

But I also understood that this was a sick game we all play in the world today. There is a finite amount of wealth and power, and we all compete for the same pool of resources. I was simply born on the other side of the fence, the team opposing Abu Sayyaf. In a parallel world, who is to say that I would not have been born in a poor Tausūg village, seeing myself as a Robin Hood–esque hero who robs wealthy foreigners to feed the poor? I do not hate Abu Sayyaf or any of the enemies I have faced on the battlefield. We are on opposing teams by dint of fate, and I sometimes sympathize about how unlucky this particular Abu Sayyaf subgroup was to kidnap my family friend and to run into me, at that particular crossroads in life, with the bandwidth and motivation to fully focus my capabilities on operating against them. I sometimes wonder whether later, when the bullets started to fly and many of them were in their final moments, they had any idea who was behind it all. I sometimes hope they bear me no ill will either. We were just born on opposing teams, and none of us really ever had a choice in the matter.

I also understood the mission. I had done my fair share of kicking in doors in Iraq, trading rounds with thugs like these. But a kidnapping situation is different from almost any other combat operation. It's a game of exploitation on both sides, an operation in which one side tries to exploit the virtues of the victim's family—their love, their loyalty, their willingness to beggar themselves in exchange for saving the victim's life, if need be—while the other side tries to exploit the kidnappers' patience, their risk tolerance, and their financial motivations. It is psychological warfare and the ultimate heads-up poker game.

The ill informed might think that my time in the Green Berets would have prepared me for Evelyn Chang's kidnapping, as such people tend to put us and other, louder organizations like the SEALs on a pedestal. It's perhaps true that no military organization in history has been better trained than the Green Berets to take advantage of whatever is at hand to exploit an enemy's weaknesses with unconventional solutions; however, ultimately the skill lies not with the individuals but with the team and the incredible resources and technology supporting us. I was nothing without the grizzled Green Beret sergeants and the depth of expertise among the elite specialists who filled the A Team's ranks.

To the degree possible, kidnappings are generally left to local police, or in some cases to civilians themselves, with the most professional crisis consulting firms usually attached to kidnap-and-ransom insurance policies. Lloyd's of London is particularly well known for having robust services and insurance policies in the space, and it is no surprise that most of the top global crisis consulting firms are headquartered around Lime Street.

The closest thing we had in the American military apparatus might have been a small subset of US Army Special Forces, ████████████ ██ ██ ██

████ in Okinawa was the highest-trained, most combat-experienced, and best-resourced ████████████████████████████████ unit in the Asia region.

This was a holdover from a time when regional commanding flag officers were called commanders in chief, before Secretary of Defense Donald Rumsfeld declared, quite correctly, that there was only one commander in chief, the President of the United States. I served on my second A Team, ODA 134, as a team leader within this unique outfit in Okinawa, under an amazing commander, Ken Gleiman, ████████ ██.

Yet in those moments of solitude in my suite at the Peninsula Hotel, I found myself wondering whether I really had what it would take to win Evelyn Chang's freedom.

I had certainly seen this kind of operation go bad. Horribly bad.

In 2009, during my last trip to Iraq, I had seen several cases in which children or aid workers or just random citizens had been snatched off the street and, despite elaborate efforts to rescue them, ultimately been killed, either in cross fire during a raid or simply slaughtered by their kidnappers, even after ransoms had been paid.

Perhaps the kidnappers had wanted to cover their tracks, or perhaps they did it out of rank sadism. Such atrocities were not at all uncommon in the chaotic environment of Baghdad in the years following the collapse of Saddam Hussein's regime. I knew that any member of Abu Sayyaf could certainly be bloodthirsty enough to kill Evelyn just for the thrill of it, if no deal could be made. They had done it to other hostages.

But when the darkness and dread really overtook me, I would conjure the face of a young boy in Iraq, a child who had been abducted and held in a cage in a brothel. I summoned the tear-filled look of joy and relief on his father's face when we helped engineer his release, and I drew some strength from that.

The boy's name was Amir. At that time, kidnapping rings had sprung up all over Baghdad and beyond, snatching up the children of people perceived to be wealthy and then ransoming them for $10,000 to $20,000. Even when they were motivated principally by greed, rather than politics, their tactics were pure terrorism.

They would threaten family members for ransom money by sending fingers, one at a time. Once they had gotten their claws into a family who was willing to pay, sometimes they never let go. It was not unusual for the same kidnappers to snatch the same victim a second time, just to squeeze more money out of a grieving family who had proven themselves willing to pay.

We in the US military were certainly aware of the fact that this evil cottage industry had sprung up in Baghdad, but as a general rule, we had pretty much decided that as a matter of official policy, it was somebody else's problem. I realize how hard-hearted this sounds, but the way we saw it was that we were the tip of the sword in Iraq, and our job was to root out the most dangerous terrorists, the leaders and subleaders of the bands who were killing American soldiers in ambushes and with suicide bombs and IEDs, and who were routinely blowing up the government officials and buildings we were sworn to protect.

Criminals may have had their tentacles in the kidnapping industry, but our official position was that we had other fish to fry. Corrupt as they were in many cases, it was the job of the local authorities to bring kidnappers to justice. Or not.

But one sunny afternoon in Baghdad, a band of kidnappers made a terrible mistake. They had planned to snatch the child of a wealthy oil baron, but they accidentally grabbed the wrong kid. They snatched Amir, the son of a powerful and influential Iraqi military colonel who had distinguished himself by working closely with the Americans since the beginning of the war in 2003. In fact, they snatched the son of the colonel in command of the vaunted Iraqi Counter Terrorism Force, our partnered tier I elite unit, the national mission force, which was headquartered with us at the secretive ███████ backwater of Baghdad International Airport (as the Viking alluded to). Our problems were his problems, so his problem became our top problem.

Suddenly, Amir's kidnapping was a priority for me, particularly since I had built a great friendship with the colonel along with his legendary operations officer, Arkan Fadhil. We were able to make an internal case for training hostage-rescue missions in a real-world environment, cast from our roles as combat advisers and trainers of the Iraqi special forces unit that was supposedly building up to this capability. No training is better than the real thing, right? At least that's how we pitched it to our commanders from the 10th Special Forces Group at the time.

The truth was that we had absolutely no idea how to handle a kidnap-and-ransom scenario. The Green Berets had trained us to handle hostage-rescue operations, sure, and we knew how to push our men through barricaded doors with flamethrowers, and to hang upside down from rooftops with explosives on the end of broom handles to detonate on windows, to go in hot from five or six entry points, swarming the house like a tidal wave crashing through room after room, to neutralize the bad guys and save the hostage. But making absolutely sure that the hostage—or kidnapping victim—made it out unscathed during the actual negotiation, well, all we knew about that was what we had learned from watching reruns of Jack Bauer in *24* or pirated copies of *The Negotiator* and *Proof of Life*.

Days went by with no progress at all, and then, almost by accident, a talented Green Beret intelligence sergeant named Ron Flick, who I worked with in my advisory team during Operation Ultimatum II—managed to turn up a lead, the name of someone suspected of being a member of the band that had snatched Amir.

In what became a round-the-clock operation, my team, largely in support of our sister team, an extraordinarily aggressive pipe-hitting group of meat-eaters at ODA 132, conducted a seemingly endless series of raids based on information gleaned from phone data that we had captured, bursting through doors, guns at the ready, every moment on the knife's edge. It's always risky bursting into a house that you know or suspect is full of bad guys, but it's even riskier in a hostage-rescue scenario. When the bad guys hear you come in, there's a serious chance that they'll murder the hostage. You can kill every terrorist in the building, and do it without losing a single man, but if your objective—the hostage—dies, it's game over and you lose. Your mission has failed. So you race to where you believe the hostage is being held, and in doing so, you leave a lot of stones unturned, a lot of doors unopened, a lot of piles of blankets and rolled-up carpets that might conceal a gunman or a bomb. It's a trade-off. You put your life and the lives of your operators at risk in order to raise the odds of survival for the hostage. You do it without thinking too much about it. That's the job. But it's always there in the back of your mind.

Our raids did not immediately win Amir's release. They did uncover a network of kidnappers, and we realized that we were dealing with a far larger and, in some ways, far more sophisticated cabal of kidnappers than we had imagined.

Tired, frustrated, and a little jumpy, we turned up the heat and pushed even harder. Once we hit the first house, we had no guarantee that word wouldn't reach the kidnappers, who might then kill Amir to save themselves. We called it "hostage-rescue mindset," very different from "direct-action mindset," which called for a more careful room-to-room clearing, killing any threat before moving on. With hostage rescue, it was about taking greater risks to get to the hostage first, as the definition of mission success was different.

Words have meaning, and the task was "rescue," not "kill or capture." One team would rest while the other scoured the streets and hit a target, then leapfrogging each other to hit the next target based on the immediate intel, day and night, without stopping, oftentimes fast-roping under night-vision goggles out of MH-60 special operations Blackhawk helicopters directly onto the rooftops of the targets. Days passed as we never let up, hitting targets around the clock, and fatigue set in as a result of lack of sleep. Slowly we began to realize that we were dealing with more than just a band of greedy thugs. We turned up evidence that linked members of the group to influential people in what was left of Iraqi society, and even links to members of the Iraqi government.

That intelligence was a bridge too far for our political handlers. In the cauldron of corruption that was the Iraqi government at the time, there were some things that American officials were willing to cast a blind eye to, and a connection between one or more of our allies in the Iraqi parliament and a cabal of child-snatching kidnappers was one of them.

We could sense that the powers that be were losing their ardor for the pursuit of Amir's kidnappers. They didn't exactly tell us to stand down, but we saw signs that larger international issues were at play and that they'd prefer we didn't get too aggressive.

That didn't stop us. By the fourth day after Amir's abduction, we were pretty much spent, virtually sleepwalking through our raids. And then, finally, we caught a break. A big one.

Our sister team, ODA 132, had rounded up a midlevel functionary in the operation. It's an immutable rule of this sort of warfare that the frontline guys—the pipe swingers who knock down doors and shoot bad guys at close range—don't do in-depth interrogations when targets are captured, but the frontline guys can ask certain "tactical" questions in an attempt to elicit a quick bit of truth amid the shock of the capture. That's a job best left to the professionals, and the US military has some very fearsome professionals with that particular skill set.

It didn't take any special skills to get this guy to spill his guts, just a hug and a bit of kindness. Almost before anyone asked him, he gave up the location of the kidnapping ring's "headquarters," which incidentally was a brothel. I was not sure if I was surprised more at the nature of the kidnapping organization or the fact that Baghdad had operating brothels at a time like this when children needed to walk over dead bodies on the way to school.

I'm not sure why it startled me so much to learn that the women played such a critical role in the operation. Maybe I still had some sexist notion that women—regardless of their profession—would be less likely than predatory men to engage in such a heinous crime as child snatching, but the more I thought about it, the more it made sense. Throughout the Middle East, and less so in much of Asia, women are virtually invisible precisely because they are considered somehow less than men. Even we Americans, who grew up in a more or less egalitarian culture, tended to look right through women dressed head to toe in burkas when we were on patrol in Iraq, despite the fact that on several occasions, women had strapped suicide vests under their garments and killed our comrades. Old prejudices die hard. Harder sometimes than soldiers.

Certainly a woman would be able to approach a child on the street without raising suspicions, drag the child into a waiting car, and make that child disappear before anyone took notice. Nobody would even notice that a kidnapping had taken place until the kidnappers, armed with telephone numbers extracted from the victim by the sex workers, called the victim's family to demand a large ransom.

It was even more exploitative than simple kidnapping to use a culture's blind spot against it, and in a way, that made the crime seem even more heinous.

Immediately, under cover of darkness in the early-morning hours, our sister team and their Iraqi counterparts launched a raid on the brothel. Amir was not there, but the clues that would ultimately lead us to him were, along with a grotesque totem of the brutality of the kidnapping ring: a tiny, child-size cage secreted in the basement of the building that had, it appeared, been occupied only recently, along with various sex tapes. Within an hour or so, I was in the building with my team, doing the tedious follow-on work of collecting intelligence by tossing the joint, which we referred to with a typical military euphemism as "sensitive site exploitation." The sister team moved on to the next target, and we happily picked up the work they'd left behind. I jumped out of our gun trucks to hustle into the building as Kevin McCaffrey, ODA 134 communications sergeant, Penn grad and future cofounder of Blackpanda, protected me behind a M134 six-barrel, air-cooled, electronically driven rotary mini-gun on top of his armored vehicle and scanned the streets for counterattack.

As I entered the building just as the sunrise peeked over the Baghdad low-rise neighborhood, and our Iraqi counterterrorist allies had rounded up the women and now had them under guard on a long couch in the main room. The women were terrified, wailing and screaming, and a belligerent junior Iraqi officer, who had been left behind as part of the three-man local partnership, was bellowing back at them, ordering them to shut up, which of course only made them howl all the louder.

Nothing useful was going to come out of the bedlam in that room. I waited for a moment, taking in the chaos, and then, in an aggressively authoritative voice I had perfected while harassing plebes back at West Point, I barked, "Shut the fuck up!" Maybe it was my forceful presence or my commanding baritone, or maybe it was just the sight of an Asian guy decked out in full battle gear and shouting in perfect Americanese, but the whole room fell into a shocked silence, long enough for me to ask the officer where his boss was. He pointed to a room upstairs, and as my men fanned out through the building to sift through every speck of dust for clues, and as the cacophony on the couch resumed, I made my way toward the boss.

I found the Iraqi captain alone in a room with a suspect, a middle-aged, overweight slob quivering in a soiled T-shirt with that look of pure, obsequious terror that all tough guys get when they know they've been caught. Looking at him cowering in a chair as the Iraqi officer loomed over him shouting questions he really didn't want answered, I could imagine this slovenly pimp doing the same thing to Amir and other captives in the basement that he did to those women on the couch downstairs.

I didn't have time to hate him for it. He had information I needed. Before I could ask my first question, the Iraqi officer leaped on him, fists flying, pummeling the pimp with all his might. It wasn't a tactic. It was beating for the sake of a beating, as if this pimp had personally offended the Iraqi captain. The jiujitsu fighter in me dove into the fray, separating them and controlling the captain until he calmed down.

I hate to say it, but the Iraqi captain's emotional, violent, unprofessional eruption had given me a card to play. As I ordered him to stand at arm's length, I began to play the "good cop" role for all I was worth. It was February, and no place on the planet feels colder than an old masonry house in the desert winter. The pimp was sweating and shivering at the same time as he sat there in his soiled underwear, so I ordered the captain to fetch him some blankets and a bit of water, and I watched as Danny Perez, ODA 134 medical sergeant, Harvard grad, and founding Blackpanda member, accompanied him to prevent another unexpected attack. With my young, talented, and very courageous female interpreter at my side, I began to speak softly, my words taking on an even more gentle tone when filtered through her lilting voice. I sidled closer to him on the couch and rested my arm on his shoulder. He revolted me, but I could feel that he was beginning to break. I asked where Amir was. He told me he didn't know. But I could see in his eyes that he was lying, and that with a little more gentle prodding, he could be persuaded to cooperate.

And then, out of nowhere, the Iraqi captain's rage erupted again. He grabbed the leg of a chair, broken off during the initial assault, and swung for the fences, striking the pimp with such force that he fractured his collarbone and damn near injured me in the process. I was furious, not just that he had brutally attacked a prisoner—a direct violation of our policy, especially after the atrocious behavior of American jailers at the notorious Abu Ghraib prison had come to light—and not just because he had grazed me with his wildly swinging billy club. No, what outraged me was that he had done it so openly, so brazenly, as if he had expected me to condone what was effectively the torture of a prisoner.

I had seen too much of that while helping manage the prisons of the Asayish secret police in Kurdistan, near the Turkish border, and I believed deeply that it fundamentally undermined what little moral justification we had as Americans in Iraq in the first place. The way I saw it, and still see it, we were no better than Saddam if we condoned torture, if we were better at all, in the end.

I'll admit that I manhandled the captain as I ejected him from the room. At least a bit of the rage that he had focused on the pimp was now smoldering in my direction. But I didn't care. I could deal with him later. I returned to the room.

No more beatings. No more threats. Just a counterfeit of kindness on my part by putting my arm around him with a blanket. Within ten minutes, this pimp and kidnapper broke down in tears, confessed, and gave up Amir's location. He was in a safe house, an obscenely ironic word for a place where a child captive was being held, and as fate would have it, it was just a few doors down the street from where he had misled our sister team. I immediately called my sister ODA 132 team's leader, Doug Peterson, over the radio with a detailed update. The team had just finished raiding the wrong place, and in moments, before I could even wipe the pimp's sweat off my uniform, our guys were already stacking up outside to raid the safe house.

I wasn't there when Amir and his father were reunited at last. I still had to clean up in the wake of my sister team's operation. But I did get to watch a video of the reunion afterward, and I can still picture it to this day. The ODA 132 medical sergeant Tony Marion held a low carry on his M4 with the suppressor attached, crouched, as our C-4 explosive charge blew the safe house door open—he charged through the door, weapon at the ready. I can still hear Amir's quavering little voice saying, "Papa?"—first as a question, and then again as a cry of joy. I can still see him running into his father's arms, burying his face in his father's chest as the Iraqi men danced and the Americans beamed, a brief moment where we thought it might actually be worth it all.

I remember thinking that the pure joy of a rescued child was, more than anything else I had ever done, what being a soldier, a Green Beret, was all about. On that day I could never imagine myself doing anything else with my life.

And then life intervened.

All these thoughts resurfaced as I lay in a king-size bed in Manila's Peninsula Hotel, torturing myself, thinking of all the ways that Evelyn Chang's rescue operation could go wrong, of all the times that they had gone wrong in Iraq, knowing that they had gone wrong just as often in the jungles of Mindanao. But as I thought about Amir, I allowed myself to think that maybe, just maybe, I had what it would take to help reunite her with her family because at one point in my life, I did run with America's best.

MANILA, PHILIPPINES

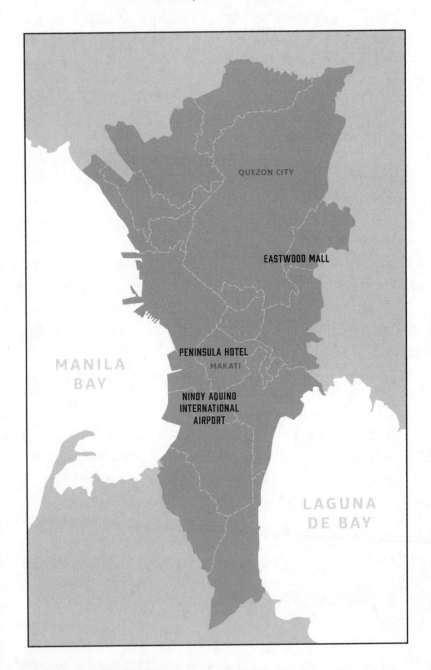

QUEZON CITY

EASTWOOD MALL

PENINSULA HOTEL

MAKATI

NINOY AQUINO
INTERNATIONAL
AIRPORT

MANILA
BAY

LAGUNA
DE BAY

Chapter 11

Kissing Her Ring

For the next several days after our meeting at the strip club, the Viking and I worked independently. I spent my days and nights sprawled out on the bed at the Peninsula Hotel. With visions of Roland's fishing-vest arsenal dancing in my head, I killed time with a little "phishing" of my own. I had the number of one of the phones the kidnappers had used to contact the Chang family in Taiwan, as they unwisely chose not to mask their caller ID, so I decided to make the best of it.

Masking my origin with VPNs and other basic cybersecurity practices, I sent out a vaguely pornographic image with an executable file hidden behind it to the phone number as an SMS that I had downloaded via a dark web marketplace site similar to the infamous "Silk Road" I had come across while refamiliarizing myself with the tech world at Palantir, which sold malware like this for a subscription fee. This is called "phishing" in cybersecurity, or "smishing" if you want to be more precise since it was sent via SMS. The image I selected was typical of the sex worker advertisements one might see in Southeast Asia, littered on the street. Sure enough, I got a bite. It had been some years since I'd taken the first university cybersecurity course ever offered, as part of my studies as a coding geek at West Point, but my recent stint at Palantir had reopened my eyes to what I could do with a keyboard and Google. Having been formally trained as a computer scientist, I have the technical confidence to figure these things out when necessary.

It's a maxim of warfare that they don't teach in military academies or on maneuvers: your enemy's most dangerous enemy is often in his own pants. When they clicked open the photo to get a better look at the women, I was able to triangulate their location and even capture their SMS, reading their shorthand Tagalog and Tausūg via Google Translate, although I was unable to grab any actionable intelligence before they wisely changed handsets after a week or so. Coupled with the Viking's human intelligence—his teams of moped-riding spies scouring the countryside around Jolo and collecting data on sightings of the out-of-place, diabetic Taiwanese factory girl with the injured wrist—I was confident that we had a reasonable lock on Evelyn Chang's precise whereabouts from mutually exclusive sources, briefly confirmed by an American signals officer whom my Palantir colleagues had reached before he was ordered to stand down from helping the rogue Gene Yu any further. I could take some comfort in that. We had operated with less in Iraq—two sworn statements to Allah—before putting all our lives on the line in a raid to capture or kill terrorists.

There wasn't much else I could take comfort in. I had already been reminded of just how maddeningly complex and potentially corrupt the byzantine world of intelligence and law enforcement was in Manila. Within days of my arrival, Richard Chang, the faux-biker patriarch of the Chang clan, had flown in from Malaysia, and I had hoped to debrief him at a ramshackle apartment in a ramshackle building in a part of town called Salcedo Village. The place had been designated as an operation center by the Philippine authorities, including the Philippine National Police's Anti-Kidnapping Group (AKG), an almost-laughably named police unit that had a reputation for being both feckless and incompetent and perhaps a bit corrupt. The AKG was sticking close to Richard, and when I got to the apartment, he was literally surrounded by surly officials and a few sour-looking police officials, from both the Philippines and Taiwan, who warily stayed on opposite sides of the room from each other, with barely any clearance or authority to work together via Interpol liaisons. These were clearly rookies at international collaboration, and they were skittish and awkward—clearly distrustful of each other—again, the fruits of having zero formal diplomacy.

They were unwelcome and rude to me, and brusquely ordered me to leave and to stay out of the situation entirely before I could even offer up that I had already pinpointed Evelyn's location via my individual cybersecurity tactics and American signals intelligence. It was clear from the get-go that I'd never be able to have a frank discussion with Richard as long as these guys were around, but I had one potential ally in the group, a bespectacled, professorial-looking Taiwanese cop by the name of Billy Huang. He, too, had concluded that the gang bang in the apartment was an obstacle to a productive exchange of intelligence that could lead to a successful plan, and he saw me as a guy he could work with, so through a series of signals and furtive whispers, we began to establish a channel behind the backs of the other officials. It wouldn't amount to much, and I think we both realized that, but at least I'd have a sense of what—if anything—the official powers that be were doing. Billy was particularly valuable in this regard since I was now openly disobeying both Taiwan and Philippine official police orders, as well as Interpol, and this line of communication played a crucial role in avoiding exposing our clandestine efforts throughout the operation.

At the time, I had hoped to find a quick solution via the Viking, pass it off, leave the country, and get back to my own sorrows and problems, but yet again, I found myself dragged in deeper, again forced to explore my own options to win Evelyn's release. It was painfully obvious to me that leaving it with the joint effort between Taiwanese bureaucratic Interpol police and junior Filipino AKG sergeants was not going to result in anything worthwhile. Most of all, I simply did not trust them.

In the meantime, the Viking had opened what amounted to another avenue, albeit littered with costume jewelry and reeking of perfume.

Her name was Nur-ana Indanan Sahidulla. She claimed to be a Sulu princess, a direct descendent of the sultans who once ruled the restive region around Jolo, back in the days before successive waves of occupation and the brutality of colonization had reduced it to a desperate, impoverished backwater and split the sultanate between eastern Malaysian Borneo and the southern Philippines islands. She called herself Lady Ann and insisted that others call her that as well. She was, in that corner of the country, a serious power broker. She was married to the then mayor of Tongkil, a small island in the Sulu Archipelago chain that Jolo Island rests firmly in the center of, and she would later serve twice as mayor herself before becoming vice-governor of the region. This incestuous and hereditary transfer of political power alongside their own privately funded armed militias within families in the provinces is why many in Manila sometimes colloquially refer to these rural governors, mayors, or even large barangay captains as "warlords." She headed the local chapter of the Red Cross, a position that afforded her even greater standing among a populace that had seen so much devastation from war and natural disasters.

She was, at that time, building a personal army, a group that later became known as the Citizen National Guard, a paramilitary organization that would pledge itself loyal to the man who would become the Philippines' authoritarian President Rodrigo Duterte. When I met Lady Ann, that army was still more like a personal bodyguard team. She had her scrapes with the law from time to time. In 2019, for example, while running for Congress, she and her husband pleaded guilty to corruption charges for failing to report a piece of property and a couple of used cars they owned. They were ordered to pay a small fine and sentenced to a year and a day in jail, though there is no record of her ever serving a minute of that sentence.

Lady Ann had a few admirable successes as well. In 2008, she was widely credited with engineering the release of three Red Cross workers—two of them foreigners—who, like Evelyn, had been kidnapped by Abu Sayyaf terrorists, and years later she played a key role in winning the release of celebrated Filipina television news-woman Ces Drilon, who likewise had been snatched by Abu Sayyaf and threatened with decapitation. Lady Ann would be criticized for her role in those events: she came under fire for giving the terror-ists what amounted to pocket money in the Red Cross case, about US$900, which she described as "money for cigarettes" and a show of "good faith."

Such transactions are really quite common in the Philippines and other hubs of kidnapping for profit. An unwritten rule states that all along the path, palms will be greased and most people tend to look the other way. It's as common and expected as tipping in an American diner. Even those in positions of authority often accept and provide such tokens while conducting their official business. Americans might naively quail at such a concept, calling it corruption, but it's a com-mon practice in the States as well, just more institutionalized. It's called lobbying. In Lady Ann's case, the criticism was muted, and in 2013, when I met her, that was all yet to happen in its entirety. She also had a glowing endorsement from the AKG, which didn't exactly fill me with confidence.

I was not prepared for the meeting. The Viking and Roland had flown her to Manila, and at the appointed time, she and her armed entourage swept into the spacious lobby of the Peninsula Hotel as if she were the queen of Siam. I remember thinking to myself that if they could have found a palanquin underneath the portico at the Peninsula Hotel, her thuggish acolytes would have carried her in on that. As it was, she settled for a grand entrance on foot.

I had to suppress a laugh as she entered. Lady Ann was a study in contradictions, a plain-looking middle-aged woman—she would have fit in on the sidelines of a middle school girls' soccer game in Cupertino—except that she was literally wrapped in what passes for the trappings of wealth in that part of the world. She wore a gray velour running suit, and she was bedecked with baubles and bracelets that jangled like a burglar alarm with every step she took. Atop her head, she wore an elaborate multicolored turban, shot through with golden threads. Completing the picture were a pair of bright white and gray New Balance running shoes. Later, Evelyn would tell me that she remembered seeing a woman of Lady Ann's exact description in the camp, freely coming and going, unlike other visitors. I tend to believe her. Lady Ann was hard to forget.

I could tell from twenty yards away that she took herself seriously, probably far too seriously, and that her entourage took her every bit as seriously as she took herself.

I glanced at the Viking and Roland. They took her seriously too. Roland was practically shivering in reverential anticipation as Lady Ann glided toward us, her hand extended so we—all three of us—could prepare ourselves for the honor of kissing it.

I did. With all the courtly deference that she demanded.

It occurred to me while I was down there, smooching her knuckle, that if all these hard-asses took her this seriously, it was a good bet that Abu Sayyaf did as well. After all, there's a thin line in these desperate places between those who sign on with organizations like Abu Sayyaf and those who cast their lot with petit potentates like Lady Ann, and I knew from my experience in the Philippines that it was not unusual to glide from one side to the other when circumstances warranted it. Lines and sides are seldom hard and fast in places like this. Your ally can be your enemy one day and your best friend the day after that.

The Viking had assured me that Lady Ann possessed standing and connections within the terrorist sphere of influence in Jolo, which we would need to begin negotiations with Evelyn Chang's kidnappers. At the very least, Lady Ann could help me with my primary objective: getting the terrorists to accept medicine for Evelyn's raging diabetes before her health deteriorated any further, and establishing some initial trust and rapport in the communication channel with a confidence-building exchange.

There would, of course, be a price. I could tell from the moment I met her that Lady Ann, despite her grand title with the Red Cross, was not the kind of person to be motivated by humanitarian impulses alone. Looking into her deep, dark eyes, I could see she was the type to weigh every angle carefully, and I quickly concluded that she had two key objectives. The first was political—she had aspirations for higher political office. Specifically, she had her sights set on running for Congress—and would later mount a bid for the Senate—so making herself indispensable in an operation to free a foreign captive would certainly burnish her credentials. I suspected that she was already imagining the headlines as we spoke.

The second objective was a bit more personal, and probably a lot more venal. As I've said before, Abu Sayyaf had turned kidnapping into a cottage industry, and despite the official position of the Philippine government that no ransom would be paid to terrorist kidnappers, that rule was honored more in the breach. Over the years, millions of dollars had been passed among many hands in a series of kidnappings, and a good portion of it had ended up sticking to the fingers of those who had played a role in the negotiations. That list included cops and soldiers, local dignitaries, high-ranking congressmen, and beyond. It was such a common practice in all facets of business, politics, and military power that it wasn't really even considered corruption. It was just a part of the cost of doing business. It was a justifiable opportunity for everybody to rob from the rich and feed the poor. I had seen a similar tolerance for profiting from terrorism in Iraq and in Kurdistan, and later on in the odd places Blackpanda found itself, including many other developing markets, so I wasn't particularly surprised to see that the practice was alive and well in the Philippines. Gold-embroidered turbans, top-shelf running shoes, and private goon squads don't come cheap.

I had concluded most of this before a word was spoken. Lady Ann's grand entrance made clear that this first meeting was not for negotiating the fine points of a rescue operation. This was a purely theatrical exercise—kind of a stock Chinese summer opera—designed to leave me in awe of her immense prestige. Given my lack of options, I pretended to be suitably impressed, but I already had my doubts.

When she spoke—finally—I found it difficult to follow her. It wasn't just that she spoke in circles, overpronouncing every English word and often choosing the wrong one, with a voice that sounded like a fly trapped under an overturned water glass. It was that every sentence seemed to begin and end with a reference to herself in the third person. Maybe that was a byproduct of her master's degree in marketing and communication, but the one language in which she seemed to be utterly fluent was the language of self-promotion.

She also appeared to be fully conversant with the daily eruptions of hyperbole about Evelyn in the Taiwanese media. Several times Lady Ann referred to the great tragedy that had befallen this Taiwanese national treasure, this Very Important Tourist who was, as the newspapers asserted, almost part of the President of Taiwan's family. Such a tragedy. Such a treasure. Clearly no price could ever be too high to win her release.

I have learned in my life that it is dangerous when people think that you have money. That is why people with real money never talk about it. And what is even more dangerous is when people *think* you have money and you don't have it.

Lady Ann left no room for me to correct her misconception. Perhaps that was intentional. It worried me, but I took some solace in her insistence that she could reach deep into the hearts of the Abu Sayyaf kidnappers and persuade them that it was in their interest to treat Evelyn with kindness—allowing the medicine to reach her, for example—and ultimately to agree to her release.

"I know these boys," Lady Ann told me. "They're my boys." They knew her, she insisted, admired her, respected her, honored her hereditary title, and would listen to her. She repeatedly portrayed herself as a "humanitarian" and never mentioned a fee, but in a culture where skimming is expected as part of the system, one seldom has to. It is a matter of saving face and elegance to keep some things unsaid.

Nothing solid came of that first meeting. That was not what it was for. That would come at a second meeting, a few days later.

It could not have been more different from the first encounter. Roland had called my hotel room early that morning, purportedly to hurry me along, and I could tell by the way that he hissed his words that he was already half-drunk at 7:00 a.m. I showered, shaved, and dressed, and then Roland, the Viking, and I were on our way to one of Manila's most desolate precincts, bound for a squalid little apartment where the meeting would occur.

The place set me on edge. Cultivated in rooms just like it in Iraq, my instincts kicked in, and I positioned myself in such a way that if something went wrong, I could get out. But my escape route would be blocked when Lady Ann and her gunsels swarmed in, this time without the faux-regal courtliness they had displayed in the lobby of the Peninsula Hotel. This time they flooded into the room with a studied air of displeasure. There was none of the grand circumlocution of that first meeting either. This time I had no trouble understanding her.

Lady Ann informed me, in no uncertain terms, that she had heard, both from her "boys" and her friends in the AKG, that the kidnappers had set a ransom of US$5 million for Evelyn's release, a staggering sum that would have been comical if a woman's life had not been hanging in the balance. She also informed me that, despite my claims to the contrary, she knew that Evelyn came from a wealthy and influential family in Taiwan and that Taiwan's national honor was at stake, and thus there was no reason on earth for the government itself not to fork over such a tiny sum, a rounding error for a government as wealthy as Taiwan's.

I tried to explain, patiently at first and then more forcefully, that the family could scrape together only US$50,000, and that even that would nearly break them. I added that not only was the government of Taiwan not going to pay any ransom, but the President himself came from a very humble financial background and was neither wealthy nor corrupt, unlike the typical political leaders across the world where wealth and power go hand in hand, even in America. I knew this because I am part of the family, and we break our backs to ensure that we are as clean as a whistle at all times, in light of the rampant historical corruption in the Kuomintang, which many historians point to as the true problem underlying its loss in the war with the communists. I wanted to make sure no one thought that anybody within two degrees of affiliation to my uncle caused any blemish of corruption on his name. Lady Ann, her nostrils flaring, her thugs getting more twitchy with every passing second, called me a liar, as her anger rose with the sense of being cheated out of her lucrative broker fees by me.

This was no longer a negotiation. It was nothing short of a shakedown, and I tried to keep my composure, as few things trigger me more as a West Pointer than to be accused of lying. Bend the rules and push the envelope? Color a little outside the lines? Every day. Play the cards you're dealt. As we say in the Green Berets, "If you ain't cheatin', you ain't tryin'" and "It pays to be a winner." But the calmer I tried to seem, the more belligerent and threatening Lady Ann and her thugs became. It suddenly crossed my mind that I could be kidnapped as well—and if they knew my real identity, an actual family member of the President of Taiwan, what price would the warlord have asked then? I felt my face become red with shame and embarrassment for not considering my own risk, unaccustomed to considering my family's status during operations. I remember scanning the room, like the operator I had been, trying to figure out which one of them I could take out first, with my bare hands, to effectuate my escape. It very nearly came to that.

At one point, one of them rushed toward me as I barked an unfriendly response to the accusation of lying, but just before we got close enough to trade blows, the Viking, displaying remarkable agility for a man of his size, got between us and literally dragged me out the door as the room descended into chaos.

Adrenaline was turning into pure rage in my veins, and the Viking and I got into a shouting match once we got back to safety at the Peninsula. He had, in my estimation, not only failed to provide us with a trustworthy ally. He and his drunken, psychopathic partner Roland had now intentionally introduced another dangerous adversary into the mix, further complicating an already intensely complicated matter. I would not only have to work against the terrorists who had kidnapped Evelyn, but I would also have to defend against the predations of Lady Ann. It was right about then that the Viking made his threat to hurl me, body and soul, off a thirty-eighth-floor balcony at the Peninsula Hotel. Right after moving a safe distance away from the windows, I effectively fired him, cutting him and Roland loose with several days still left on their contract.

To his credit, the Viking took the news in stride, and cooler heads prevailed. We still had a bit of a bond between us: we spoke the same operator language, I believed he had been at ███████ back in the day, and we worked together throughout the rest of the operation, pro bono, with the Viking feeding me intel and advice as it came to him and providing secure transport from time to time.

Roland displayed less equanimity. Late that night, as I tossed and turned in my bed, the telephone rang. Roland had apparently kept on pounding back the drinks after our disastrous meeting with Lady Ann and her cohort. "I'm going to slit your throat as you sleep. You can't hide from me in my town. You owe us that Taiwan money," he hissed into the phone before hanging up. It was the first thing Roland had ever said to me that I believed without reservation.

Great, I thought to myself. *I have no plan, no allies, and a whole new clown car full of enemies. And now I have to find a new place to stay.*

On the plus side, at least my mother didn't know about any of this.

ZAMBOANGA, PHILIPPINES

Chapter 12

Strikes and Spares

My arm reared back, my eyes focused on the seven-ten split at the far end of the lane, and when, at just the precise moment, I let go of the ten-pound ball, it was with just enough delicate spin to nail the seven and send it hurtling like an air-to-ground missile, obliterating the ten pin.

Look at me, I thought. *All of a sudden, I'm a little Big Lebowski.*

The guy behind the counter who rents the shoes that stink of mold and antifungal powder gave me an admiring glance. Not too shabby for someone who never bowls. But what the hell else did I have to do?

It's not like I could go back to my room in the plush Peninsula Hotel and wallow in my sorrows. My entire plan to rescue Evelyn Chang, such as it was, lay in shambles at the feet of the Viking, Lady Ann, and Roland. In fact, I was ready to give up and had begun to prepare to fly back to Taipei, meet Angela, and confess that I had failed. I tried to distract and console myself that there was still a chance that I could catch my Hong Kong friends on the Nepal trip, since they had just arrived in Kathmandu and were acclimatizing to the altitude and purchasing last-minute gear.

I had immediately checked out of my luxurious digs at the Peninsula after Roland threatened to slit my throat in my sleep in the middle of the night. Indeed, the coming weeks would be spent on a grand tour of every cheap Airbnb in the greater Manila area, using them as impromptu personal safe houses, just like how insurgent leaders did in Iraq by moving their bed-down locations every night to keep us on our toes. I hadn't gotten much rest the night before. It's hard to sleep when you've got one eye open all night and both ears trained for the telltale sound of gunmetal rubbing up against the inside of a nylon fishing vest.

To be honest, I believed the game was over, that it would be impossible to steer a course around the obstacle that Lady Ann and her personal army had become. Not to mention Roland. And my near-daily communications with the Chang family back in Taiwan were convincing me that things were getting worse for Evelyn. They'd send me links to videos of Tsai Cheng-Yuan, that insipid Taiwanese lawmaker who never met a camera crew he didn't try to ambush.

He had seen in the Chang case an opportunity to cast himself as a real hero, a tough guy. Because he also saw himself as a legitimate rising star in my uncle's party, he milked the tragedy of her kidnapping for all it was worth, insisting that the President wasn't doing nearly enough to rescue Evelyn, who was—Tsai insisted, against all evidence—a close friend of my uncle's, practically a member of the family. It was a twofer, as far as Tsai was concerned. My uncle was, of course, constrained by the strictures of his office. There was no official channel between Taiwan and the Philippines that he could use to leverage her release. The complex nature of international relations in Asia, with the stark shadow of mainland China looming over everything, made direct action or any official coordination impossible. Tsai knew that, of course. But it didn't stop him from casting himself as the Lone Avenger of Taiwan's national honor, real "I alone can fix it" stuff, to borrow a Trumpism that Americans might be familiar with, aimed at the same target audience and delivered with the same bluster.

It didn't matter to him that every time he opened his mouth, he was endangering Evelyn even further and strengthening the hands of both

Abu Sayyaf and Lady Ann. At some point, I realized, we'd have to find a way to muzzle Tsai and a way to sideline Lady Ann.

Even more alarming were the reports I was getting about Evelyn herself. Her family reported to me that their brief telephone conversations with her—her captors would force her to call and plead desperately for the ransom money—were often punctuated by Evelyn's cries of fear as her captors intimidated her with their bolo knives to her throat and guns to her head. Despite their brutality, or perhaps because of it, the physically and psychologically fragile factory girl was beginning to see her kidnappers not as her tormentors but as her allies. Stockholm syndrome is a common phenomenon among captives, and there was mounting evidence that Evelyn was starting to suffer from it.

She had begun to see her captors as her salvation, even referring to one of my old adversaries, Sihata Latip, the man in charge of the band of thugs torturing her, as her "big boss." She would soon come to imagine that her own family possibly stood as an obstacle to her salvation, and I began to fear that she wasn't just deteriorating but disintegrating, and that it would be only a matter of time before he and his increasingly frustrated gang came to see her as a liability.

As dismal as the circumstances seemed in this moment, we suddenly had some cause for hope.

In the depths of my near despair and killing time before heading off to the airport, my cell phone rang. It was a guy I had met recently named Joe Felter, an adviser to Palantir, a West Pointer, Stanford professor, and a former Green Beret colonel himself, a guy who knew the lay of the land in the Philippines. He put me in touch with the godfather of his own children, Lieutenant Colonel Dennis Eclarin. Dennis was, I had been told, the one guy in all of the Philippines that I could absolutely rely on, a key officer in the Philippine Scout Rangers, a 1993 graduate of West Point, a soldier through and through. Felter told me that Dennis was one of the few officers in that country with a reputation for being flawlessly professional and completely incorruptible. Dennis himself later humbly regaled me with the story of how he'd gained the respect of his colleagues years earlier when, during a failed military coup in the 2000s, one of several that shook the country at the time, he reluctantly strode into the Glorietta Mall in downtown Manila and gently faced down his former comrades, speeding an end to that uprising.

Dennis was also stealthy as hell. He had insisted that our first meeting be clandestine, so for an entire day I hung around that brightly lit bowling alley and a TGIF restaurant at the newly built Eastwood Mall, nearby at the edge of Quezon City, waiting for him to show. After all I had heard about Dennis and the Scout Rangers' jungle-warfare exploits, I half expected that when he finally did arrive, he'd suddenly emerge from a bush in full sniper ghillie suit gear with camouflage paint masking his face. You can imagine my surprise when a slightly short, slightly paunchy middle-aged man, looking more like a gentle high school guidance counselor than a trained killer, sidled up to me at the food court, ordered a dank cup of coffee in one of the cheap white plastic cups ubiquitous in the Philippines, introduced himself, and told me, "West Pointer to West Pointer, I will help you. This is a West Point thing."

Despite Dennis's appearance, I could feel West Point in him. He had that ineffable sense about him, a kind of preternatural calm and depth, an almost-paternal air that inspired confidence. Based on the little he had been told about the case, he had already developed a kind of empathetic attachment to Evelyn Chang, whom he saw as an ordinary person cruelly plunged into horribly extraordinary circumstances. Because Dennis, too, came from a modest background, he seemed to feel a deep connection to her. It was the idea of defending common people that had drawn him to the military in the first place. He began to refer to Evelyn affectionately as "the factory girl," borrowing the term from the title of a bestselling book he was reading about the travails of a struggling young female factory worker in China.

Dennis told me that he understood the danger of the situation and pledged on his honor as a West Pointer that he would do all he could personally do to help. His ace in the hole, he explained, was another legendary Philippine Scout Ranger officer—who was introduced to me simply as "Nick," and it crossed my mind that his work must be so secretive that even his nickname needed a nickname—who was not only already on the ground in Jolo but had two human intelligence assets inside the terrorist camp. Nick was on loan to the NICA as an intelligence operative and had been posing as an engineer working at a local construction company, responsible for paying protection money to Abu Sayyaf, and thus developing relationships inside the organization. And his sources were painting a picture that confirmed my worst fears.

"Our factory girl is not in good shape," Dennis told me.

As I'd expected, Dennis reported she had barely received any medical care for her broken wrist—snapped during the brutal abduction—nor had she received medication for her diabetes. Dennis also confirmed my hunch about her psychological deterioration. That was no surprise. Stronger people than Evelyn Chang had been broken by the kind of relentless physical and emotional torture she had been subjected to. It was practically a miracle that she had survived this long.

We also saw signals that the ongoing ordeal was taking its toll on the terrorists. Nick's sources in the camp had picked up rumblings among some that it was nearly time for them to cut their losses. They'd done it in the past. Out of frustration or fear, or even boredom, they'd executed troublesome captives, decapitating them and then posting the executions on social media. Others in the camp, those with slightly cooler heads, were also looking for a way to get rid of Evelyn, Nick's sources told him, and they were sketching out a plan to sell her to the main element of Abu Sayyaf at its headquarters. That core unit, led by the one-armed Radullan Sahiron, with his white horse that he supposedly rode around, was deep in the mountains of Patikul to the north, an area so remote that General John J. Pershing himself could not penetrate it when he went to war against these same people's ancestors, so impenetrable that we never advised the Armed Forces of the Philippines to mount an assault into that area when most of the Abu Sayyaf leadership retreated there following Operation Ultimatum. Hidden in that redoubt was a far more cold-blooded and larger group of over five hundred true believers. Nick didn't have to tell me the last part. I already knew it. If they got their hands on Evelyn, it would be almost impossible to rescue her.

No one needed to say it out loud. We were running out of time. At least now I had friends I could rely on. With the added benefit that, as crazy as Roland might be, he wasn't crazy enough to come after me with that bowie knife of his when I was standing shoulder to shoulder with some of the best soldiers in the country. I took some comfort in that.

The next thing I knew, I was sitting next to Dennis on a puddle jumper, making the rough descent into what remained of the Zamboanga International Airport.

We didn't speak much as Dennis hustled me past the pitiful crowd of beggars and freelance porters, through the dilapidated off-white one-story building with peeling paint that passed for the airport's main terminal, a place that looked for all the world like a cheap tiki-torch motel that had seen better days in some Florida backwater. Dennis warily scanned the mob. I understood why.

The last time I had strutted through this airport, I had been in full uniform with captain's bars on my collar, appearing less as an individual man and more as a symbol of the power and might of the United States of America. My uniform had been a shield, and behind it were a crew of other intimidating American soldiers and an even larger entourage of Philippine military and police, with their up-armored vehicles and bristling automatic weapons. I had noted the hundreds of eyeballs watching us, but it did not even cross my mind that we faced much risk, and I had felt reasonably safe with all that backup around me: a detachment of US Marines, armed to the teeth, escorted by a convoy of Philippine military.

This time at the same airport, I was just an overdressed foreigner flaunting apparent wealth, at least relative to the other civilians there, just as Evelyn Chang had been in eastern Malaysian Borneo. And that made me a potentially lucrative target. Dennis did his best to shield me from prying eyes as we hurriedly slipped into a waiting car and rattled off toward Zamboanga.

I had not seen the place in eight years or so. In the interim, it had suffered greatly, from nature and from human nature. Typhoon Yolanda had torn through the whole region, and it seemed to have wreaked its greatest havoc on Zamboanga, tearing its pitiful buildings to shreds and devastating its infrastructure. It was no surprise that in the poverty, despair, and ruin left in Yolanda's wake, Abu Sayyaf had attempted to support a larger Muslim rebellious political organization, the Moro National Liberation Front (MNLF), with its grip on the city. As noted earlier, terrorist organizations always find a way to exploit misfortune, posing as saviors, providing a bit of aid to desperate people in exchange for power. And while it was a shocking surprise, it was not implausible that the modern-day Moros had taken the opportunity to challenge Manila's tenuous control on the city, launching a fierce, days-long battle to liberate it from the Christian oppressors. I had heard about the battle, of course, how it had been cast as the most extensive and deadly street-to-street fighting in the Philippines since World War II, though I had spent enough time in the country to take that assessment with a grain of salt. There is a tendency in the Philippines, and in most under-developed countries, to romanticize even minor military engagements, to portray every skirmish as the Battle of Thermopylae and turn every inept commander into a modern-day Leonidas. I had expected that to be the case with the Battle of Zamboanga, too, but I was wrong.

Buildings on every street that had hosted ground-zero combat showed the scars of a battle that was as savage and deadly as anything I had seen in my days in Sadr City. The buildings at ground zero of the Battle of Zamboanga looked like swiss cheese blocks as the Scout Rangers and the MNLF plus Abu Sayyaf fought in close urban combat for weeks. But the real scars were carved into the muddy paths that cut through the refugee shantytown that had grown up at the edge of the city. They were etched in the faces of the little children, naked and filthy, splashing in the fetid pools of water that bred not just malarial mosquitoes but the contagion of rage and despair. The next generation of insurgents and kidnappers were already hatching on the corpse of the last great battle to contain them.

It may have been overly sentimental of me, but as we stopped and observed the camp like tourists visiting the zoo—rows of makeshift tents, little more than old tarps hung carelessly, and the street, if you could call it that, little more than a sea of trash—I couldn't help but feel a sense of failure and loss. If the mission that had first brought me to the Philippines had succeeded, if we had accomplished something meaningful in the global War on Terror rather than futilely wasting blood and treasure in untold amounts, there might have been no Battle of Zamboanga. There would not have been peace, and there certainly wouldn't have been prosperity—that was too much to hope for—but this poisonous level of devastation might have been avoided, if only for a time. What's more, if we had succeeded, if Operation Ultimatum had killed the three key leaders when we had the chance, perhaps Evelyn would never have been kidnapped. I reflected again how strategically pointless all American military efforts had appeared to be during my era, not just in the Middle East but also here in the southern Philippines. War is the most expensive thing that human beings have ever invented.

But my whole life has been a story of second chances, and I began to believe that I was being given another chance to play a role in bringing this band of killers and kidnappers a measure of justice, as well as helping a family friend in need. And not just a second chance to rectify unfinished business, perhaps, but a chance to close an unfinished chapter in my own confused past. Nothing I had ever done while serving in uniform seemed to have resolved into a positive outcome, despite all the overdone backslapping in the States, and perhaps this was my chance to tie it off in my own small way.

For the next several days, Dennis, Nick, and I huddled in a slapdash hut, a rickety NICA safe house framed by banana tree logs and surrounded by corrugated tin walls to obstruct observation from the main road, and began to sketch out a serious plan to rescue Evelyn.

The first order of business was to remove the two thorns in our side: Tsai, the loudmouthed lawmaker from Taipei, and Lady Ann. Tsai ended up being less of a problem than we had feared. We simply instructed the Chang family to let Tsai know in no uncertain terms that if he didn't shut up, the entire family would go to the press and tearfully accuse him of exploiting the tragedy for his own perfidious political objectives. Even a Harvard graduate like Tsai could grasp the terrible optics of being publicly reviled by the grieving family, and so, after apologizing to the family—admitting that "I guess I've seen too many action movies"—Tsai withdrew from the public eye, at least as far as the Evelyn Chang story was concerned. With Tsai muzzled, stories in the Taiwanese press about Evelyn Chang being a heartbeat away from the presidency slowed to a trickle, and predictably, the price that Abu Sayyaf was demanding fell precipitously, dropping to US$3 million. It was still much more than the Chang family could afford, but as far as we were concerned, it was progress.

Neutralizing Lady Ann took a bit more cunning. At my behest, we concocted a plan to use Nick's assets in the Abu Sayyaf camp to plant a false rumor that Lady Ann had already been paid a significant deposit of US$50,000 to secure Evelyn's release, and that she was holding out on Abu Sayyaf. There wasn't a word of truth in it, but the terrorists believed it, and that was what mattered. I wasn't there when it happened, but I have it from the Scout Rangers that the next time Lady Ann met with Abu Sayyaf, those blindingly white and gray running shoes of hers got quite a workout as she and her entourage fled for their lives.

That would be the last we'd hear of Lady Ann in connection with the case.

With those two obstacles removed, Dennis, Nick, and I turned our attention to developing a scheme first to reduce the ransom further and then to secure Evelyn's release. The plan we came up with was both simple and elegant. We would arrange to have the terrorists meet with members of the Scout Rangers at a neutral location, perhaps a local mosque or the home of a local imam. Then we'd hand them a bag of money, they'd turn over Evelyn, and, before they could make it back to camp, we'd ambush them and snatch back the cash.

There was one wrinkle. In addition to the dwindling amount of cash that Abu Sayyaf was demanding for Evelyn, the terrorists also wanted us to provide them with what likely amounted to bomb-making materials, specifically the kind of higher-end electronics that you used to be able to buy at any electronics store in Cupertino. But there were no such stores in Jolo, and the Abu Sayyaf's low education levels revealed their lack of confidence in securing these basic items on their own. The Green Beret in me bristled at the idea of giving these terrorists anything that could be used to make a bomb, no matter how innocuous or otherwise easily available those components might be. It was a matter of principle.

Eventually, Dennis and Nick persuaded me to go along with the plan. I agreed, with the idea that I would help design and participate in the execution of the ambush. Looking back, I realize how little enthusiasm my Scout Ranger friends had for that notion and how they simply nodded their heads at me, with no intention of allowing me to participate.

Whatever else they were, they were still loyal Filipino soldiers, and the idea of having a foreigner on the battlefield within their country was still, for them, a major stumbling block. It didn't matter whether they believed that I could carry out the mission; it didn't matter that I had done it many times in the past. I was just a foreign civilian. I understood that. I had a vested interest in bringing down the terrorist band, but it was admittedly a matter of self-interest, as I had not yet fully shed my identity as a Green Beret and it felt damn good, imagining I was playing for the same team again after all those years of loss and anger. But their interest was personal too. This was their country. This was their fight.

We'd have time, I thought, to reach an accommodation over the role I would play in the actual operation. For the moment, at least, I felt a twinge of optimism, a sense that maybe, just maybe, we were moving closer to our objective.

And then my telephone rang. I didn't even have to look. I already knew, just as I had on that sidewalk in Hong Kong a few weeks earlier. It was my mother.

IRBIL, KURDISTAN

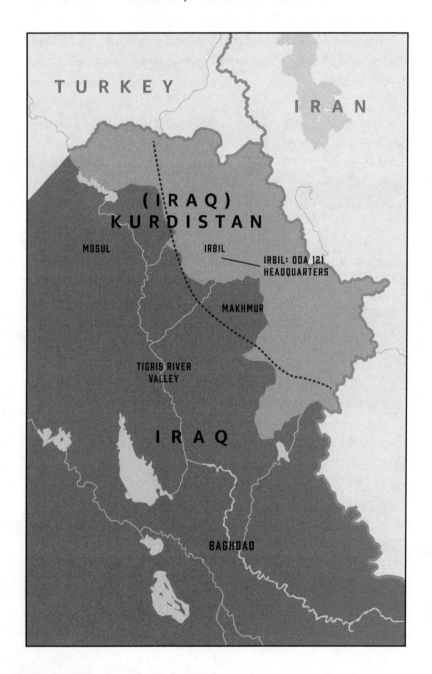

Chapter 13

The Streetlights Came On

I hadn't exactly lied to my mother. I had just sort of judiciously omitted certain key details in our occasional conversations since I had left Taipei. This was a skill I had begun to develop as a sullen teen in Cupertino and had honed to a fine art by the time I first deployed to Iraqi Kurdistan, telling her throughout that entire year that I was safely in Okinawa. And so it wasn't really my fault that when she reached me at the hooch of a safe house in Zamboanga, she thought I was living the life of a flat-broke party boy in the urban wilds of Hong Kong.

I had thought about coming clean, letting her know that her son had been secretly negotiating with duplicitous local potentates, dangerous psychopaths in fishing vests, eccentric Nordic mercenaries, and rogue factions of the Philippine military, all in a bid to engineer the release of Evelyn Chang. Then I pictured her, standing there with her lips pursed, her hands on her hips, a look of anger—and worse, of fear—in her eyes, and I decided that discretion was the better part of valor. I wasn't the only one cowed by the notion of my mother's anger. Angela Chang, who had been holding up heroically through every crushing twist and turn since Evelyn's abduction, was every bit as terrified of my mother's anger if she discovered the truth. Angela had even reached out to plead with me to do whatever my mother demanded, in order to keep the illusion alive. Her fears were not misplaced; it has been a decade since these events, and my mother has only very recently forgiven Angela.

My mother demanded that I immediately pack a bag with a good suit, hop the first flight from Hong Kong, and be ready for a job interview that she had used all her connections to arrange. The role was a senior position at a local Taiwanese semiconductor company, a far cry from the exciting job I had with Palantir, one of the prestige players in the global tech world. It felt like a major step down for a former up-and-coming master of the universe in the world of investment banking, far too provincial for a guy who saw himself playing in the major leagues. I would never have considered interviewing for it on my own. But my mother demanded, and so, convincing myself that I was doing it to protect the integrity of the mission, I meekly obeyed.

I was angry at myself, humiliated. It felt as if I were a kid back in Cupertino again, as if the streetlights had just come on and I had to sullenly trudge home or risk my mother's ire. That wasn't even the worst of it. I had to tell Dennis and Nick that I was leaving. I did my damnedest to convince them that I was only going to be gone for a day or two, a few days at most, and that it was essential that I do so to maintain the secrecy of the operation, but I could see that they didn't believe me when I channeled the ghost of another old West Pointer, Douglas MacArthur, and promised that I, too, would return.

And why would they believe me? MacArthur aside, the history of the Philippines is a history of foreigners showing up, making grand promises, and then vanishing as soon as the going gets rough. The expectation of abandonment and betrayal by big-talking foreigners is woven deeply into the DNA of every Filipino, and neither Dennis nor Nick had any reason to believe that I was any different. I knew at that moment that our mission—which had narrowly survived the machinations of Lady Ann, the danger posed by Roland, and the spectacularly threatening breach with the Viking—was at its gravest moment of peril so far, all because I didn't know how to say no to my mother.

As a Green Beret, the one thing you learn above all is that the most lethal weapon at your disposal is the trust of local, indigenous partners. Forget all the images from the special forces shoot-'em-ups you've spilled your popcorn over at the local cineplex, all those scenes of stealthy operatives rappelling down the side of a building, kicking in a window, and barging in, guns blazing. Leave that stuff to the movie stars of ███████████ and the ghosts of ███████████. Sure, we do those things from time to time, but that's not really the job. The job is building trust and rapport with your partners, making them understand that their fight is your fight, and that you'll be standing right there with them, every step of the way. It is about twelve good men parachuting behind enemy lines and suddenly turning themselves into a force of five hundred with the immediate training and creation of the local militia—what you might, in the private sector, call an excellent return on investment.

I will never forget the looks on their faces as I took my leave of Dennis and Nick. They wouldn't have mocked me for my meek deference to my mother. Filipino culture is, as others have noted, steeped deeply in Latin traditions, but there is a strong undercurrent of Confucianism, mixed with other Southeast Asian influences, and filial piety is an unquestioned value. I wish they had mocked me, because that would have meant that we still shared enough of a bond for me to be the butt of a joke. There were no jokes, just the cold, blank looks of two men who believed that they were about to be abandoned, that after all the risks they had taken to join this mission, out of pure charity, they were about to be ditched.

Nothing I could say or do would have changed their minds about me, short of telling my mother to cancel the job interview. I could see it in their eyes, and it cut me like a knife. I had seen that look before, etched on the weathered face of an ancient peshmerga warlord in Kurdistan, as he slowly recuperated from his own wounds and mourned the death of his youngest son. The son had been cut in half by automatic rifle fire during a mission that neither of them would have undertaken had I not been "called away on business" that time, too, abandoning them, at least in their eyes.

The warlord's name was Mohammed Tayib. I called him Colonel Tayib, and to this day, I might pull out my black-and-white-checkered Kurdish scarf when the wind blows cold on occasion, as if needing a reminder of my time with him. I do not. He's never far from my thoughts for too long.

Tayib was an aristocratic man who lived in a palatial home in Irbil, a member of the officer class in a place that still valued such things. In the 1980s, he had distinguished himself as an intelligence officer in Saddam Hussein's war against Iran. When that war ended and Saddam turned brutally against his own citizens, reserving the worst of his rage for the restive Kurdish population in the north, Tayib and his sons fought valiantly against him. Like all Kurds—a nation of thirty million people spread across Iraq, Iran, Turkey, and Syria, loathed and feared by all four governments—Tayib yearned for an independent Kurdish state. He fought side by side with the Americans to topple Saddam, joining the 10th Special Forces Group as they approached Baghdad from the north while the famed 3rd Infantry Division's "Thunder Run" blasted in from the south, casting his lot with the Americans in the hope that someday, with our help, a real, autonomous, free, and independent Kurdish state would emerge.

His ways, of course, were not our ways. His sprawling home was all the proof one needed that he didn't have the same aversion to plundering his adversaries as the Americans professed to have, and there were times when Tayib cast not just a blind eye but an approving one on his men as they brutalized a prisoner. He would be appropriately contrite when, after we came across these beaten and traumatized prisoners, I chastised him for it—most of the time, anyway.

I had a deep respect for Mohammed Tayib. He had stood up when a lot of men didn't, and he had made sacrifices that would have flattened a lesser man. You could see his struggles etched in his deeply lined and weathered face. You could see his pride, and you could see his pain.

His two oldest sons had both been killed in combat early in the battle against Saddam's army, and he had watched them die, as he had watched his brothers die during the war with Iran. There were other scars on his soul as well. One night, in a cloud of sweet-scented smoke from a hookah, over kebabs and couscous, I listened, rapt, as Tayib recounted in excruciating detail the horrors he had witnessed and endured during the infamous Halabja Massacre, when Saddam used chemical weapons to kill thousands upon thousands of innocent Kurdish civilians. Maybe that was why Tayib was so indulgent when it came to his last remaining son, a voluble, lovable young boy named Ibrahim.

Ibrahim was animated and funny, and his father doted on him. I can't tell you how many times Mohammed Tayib and I were engaged in some serious official strategic or tactical meeting, and Ibrahim, who was there ostensibly to pour chai into elegant little teacups adorned with golden leaves, would interrupt us, challenging his father—and me—by sketching out some elaborate and usually ridiculous theory about how we could better confront our enemies. I loved the adoring exasperation that Tayib revealed in those moments. He was what a commander should be: a father.

He also had a kind of charisma and a talent for building an army out of nothing, simply because he himself was so inspiring. Once, while bouncing down a deserted sheep track in the middle of Kurdish nowhere, Tayib suddenly stopped the truck and strutted purposely toward a figure in the distance, a young shepherd he had spotted. I could see them speaking together for a few moments, and then Tayib strutted back, beaming, announcing that he had just gained a recruit for our war against the terrorists.

They say that a US Army Special Forces officer is only as good as his indigenous allies. I was a much better officer, and maybe a much better man, because of my friendship with Tayib.

But then came the day when our bond was tested. It was the summer of 2007, a particularly hot summer, and not just in terms of the scorching sun and weather. Surprisingly well-equipped and well-financed terrorists had been raising hell all over the shattered country, and we had gathered information that led us to one of the middlemen funneling money to the insurgents. Stop the middleman, and we would effectively choke off the resources, at least locally, and at least for a while. Armies don't always march on their stomachs. Sometimes they march on their wallets.

The problem, as is so often the case in that region, was that the so-called financiers had been clever enough to develop ties with both sides. Even our most dedicated local allies were not immune to the siren song of surreptitious cash. As my wise and grizzled team sergeant wryly noted, even the venerable Tayib was vulnerable to temptation. After all, he hadn't built his palatial home by selling Kurdish scarves on Amazon. And frankly, why not? He was not being paid any meaningful wage for the sacrifices he made to fight on behalf of his impoverished Kurdish nation, and such "tips" kept the lights on, not just for himself, but for his peshmerga unit as well.

Sure enough, when we raided the financier's house—kicking down the door, seizing dozens of shopping bags crammed with cash, and taking him into custody—Mohammed Tayib became, for the first time, a reluctant ally. We had figured out another way to leverage the Kurds to help the effort to the south, namely, by way of their prisons and justice system, which was not as easily corrupted as the system of our Arab partners to the south. Other sister 10th Group Special Forces teams began sending their most valuable captured terrorists to our so-called Irbil Hostel, where we would coordinate with our Asayish secret police counterparts to throw them into formidable prisons, trusting that they would not be released the next day after a payment under the table to the judge. But Tayib insisted that the financier not be thrown into a dismal Kurdish prison to await trial. In fact, he insisted that the financier not be tried at all, despite the overwhelming evidence against him. He also insisted that the money—worth about US$30,000—be turned over to him.

I resisted. I'm not naive, and I've never been a Boy Scout, but the taint of corruption offended me. In the end, though, I had no choice but to comply. I did express my outrage in an effort to placate my team, which openly and angrily protested my decision. To drive home my displeasure, I withdrew from Tayib. My withdrawal was meant to be short lived; eventually, I knew, he and I would again be working shoulder to shoulder, but perhaps by then he would understand that there were certain red lines that he was not to cross. Not with me, not with any American officer. None of us could be seen condoning corruption. Again, I look back today and realize this is simply viewed as a formal part of the unwritten compensation system, just like tipping at American restaurants and bars, as government salaries were absurdly insufficient.

Before I could restore my ties with him, Mother called, in a manner of speaking. In this case, "Mother" was the brass in Mosul, a harrowing three-hour drive away through IED alleys. The US was at that time in the first stages of what was called "The Surge," an influx of tens of thousands of freshly added US troops to an Iraq-wide campaign to drive back the insurgents long enough to figure out a way to extricate ourselves from what was then a five-year-old war. General David Petraeus was about to testify before Congress about initial progress of The Surge, and the backroom brass in the Pentagon wanted to ensure that no embarrassing counteroffensive happened while he was testifying. So ODA 121 was summoned away from Irbil and sent out to the hinterlands on a series of pretty routine missions in an area called the Za'ab Triangle, along the Tigris River. These missions could easily have been conducted by any infantry unit, anywhere in-country. We were not hitting curated and vetted targets based on our own internal intelligence but rather following spurious leads simply to keep up the action and keep the bad guys hidden and quiet. It seemed to me to be a waste of all the special forces training we had received, but my role was not to question why. My team loudly and incessantly complained that the whole operation was an unsophisticated squandering of our unique capabilities, to be used as such a crude hammer. But we had our role to play in ensuring that Petraeus did not get upstaged by an outbreak of headline news while testifying before Congress, so we went out to smash doors at a breakneck pace, to keep the bad guys down. The whole strategy, if you could call it a strategy, was this—a good offensive is the best defense; they can't hit you while you're hitting them.

And so, without so much as a farewell nod to Mohammed Tayib to drive home my displeasure, I went south, to partner with another pesh-merga unit we had helped establish in a small town called Makhmur in the Za'ab Triangle region.

I knew I'd be back. Tayib did not. As far as he was concerned, I had abandoned him.

We were gone for three weeks.

Two days after our return to Irbil, I received a shocking phone call. Without notifying me, a US infantry company commander based in Mosul had acquired a piece of intelligence about some insurgents nearby and had decided to reach out to the nearest Iraqi Kurdish army unit for a combined operation in the middle of the afternoon, to "help stand up the Iraqi army." At the time, there had been a shift in thinking among the planners in the conventional US Army. They had noted the success of Green Beret units in standing up local forces but lacked anything resembling a sophisticated understanding of how complicated and demanding the task was. They just haphazardly mimicked our carefully crafted structure and detailed strategies, perfected over decades of similar work all over the world, assuming that they could just toss a wildly disparate collection of regular soldiers from a host of units into a team like ingredients in a blender, push the button, and expect a cohesive, multiethnic fighting force to pour out. To that end, they began blindly reaching out to any available Iraqi partner unit for "capacity-building" purposes. The results were predictable. The military term of art for it is a "clusterfuck."

The nearest unit was Tayib's, so this captain, who knew virtually nothing about Tayib or his men, dragooned my partner. Even now, all these years later, I'm still angry about that. I view it as a stunning example of the corrosive politics at play within the American military, at that time in Iraq, when there was much "mission stealing" between the conventional Army and unconventional Special Forces.

As I was not the battle-space commander of Mosul, we had to request via our 10th Special Forces Group commanders and receive approval from the conventional infantry colonel to enter Mosul to conduct a hit. If we contributed too much precise intelligence about the whereabouts and nature of the target we had painstakingly hunted down through back-alley meets with informants in the Irbil bazaar, or collected during one of our many meetings with imams out in the countryside while walking with their goats, or the endless hours sitting on cushions getting wired on sugar-infused chai, then the regular infantry, looking to burnish their reputations and maybe advance a few careers at the expense of the ill-regarded and cowboy Green Berets, would steal our missions and hit them before we got to the target, claiming the glory for the capture. Think of it as the equivalent of a senior business partner poaching your client that you curated for months after you were required to make the introduction for approval to move forward with the deal. Repeatedly.

Later on, I learned to soothe the fragile egos of conventional infantry officers by allowing their men to participate when we went after our highest-profile targets, so that the commanders could claim credit as part of their career-promotion track. I learned not to care if they took the credit. I just cared that we were able to do our jobs. When I say that I know that the Mosul-based infantry commanders were aware that Tayib's unit was with the lone US Army Special Forces team in Irbil, they also knew that we were otherwise engaged.

And so without so much as a "Mother, may I?" this captain requested that Tayib's unit enter the volatile southeastern part of Mosul, an area called "Palestine" because, like that restive region of another Middle Eastern region, it was seething and often dangerous. It had been decided that Palestine needed to be tamed. The area had become too hot to patrol and needed a conventional invasion, to be retaken street by street like the pitched battles of Fallujah. There were pockets and neighborhoods like this all over Iraq's cities in 2007, and Palestine was one of the hotter areas of Mosul. We referred to these areas as "denied territory," a term I always disliked, as I believed it simply meant that we needed to enter with more combat power. There wasn't anywhere on earth that could truly deny American military might if the requisite strength and resources were allocated appropriately.

So this infantry commander called up Tayib and sent him into Palestine as the vanguard, then hung back to see what would happen. It was a slaughter.

Tayib was leading, as usual and against my advice, as he should have been centered more safely as the commander. He was at the head of his column of two hundred men when the first IED exploded. His son Ibrahim was at his side, and reports could not tell if the blast tore that young boy in half or if it was the tandem PKM 7.62mm machine-gun fire raining down on the patrol from all angles. For the third time in half a dozen years, Mohammed Tayib watched a son die in front of his eyes. A burst of machine-gun fire strafed the streets, and four rounds tore into Tayib's chest and abdomen. They should have been lethal wounds. Miraculously they weren't, and Mohammed Tayib survived. Some of him, anyway.

It took many months for Tayib to recuperate. But he never recovered. Gone was that wise and knowing sparkle in his eyes, that spark of leadership and dignity in his crooked smile. He became a shadow of the man he had once been. When I went to visit him in his hospital bed in the operating room of the makeshift local Irbil hospital, I was one of the first to be allowed to see and speak with Tayib. I rushed to his side. I asked why he had done it, why he had led his men into that killing field.

"I thought you had abandoned me, and I need American support," he said.

The accusatory look in his eyes cut through me like a knife. I never wanted to see that look on any man's face again.

But then I did. As I made my way from the safe house to the airport in Zamboanga, I saw the same look in Dennis's and Nick's eyes, and it haunted me. I would have done anything, anything, to erase that look. Even, as it turned out, if it meant making one of the poorest decisions I've ever made in a lifetime full of bad choices.

TAIPEI, TAIWAN

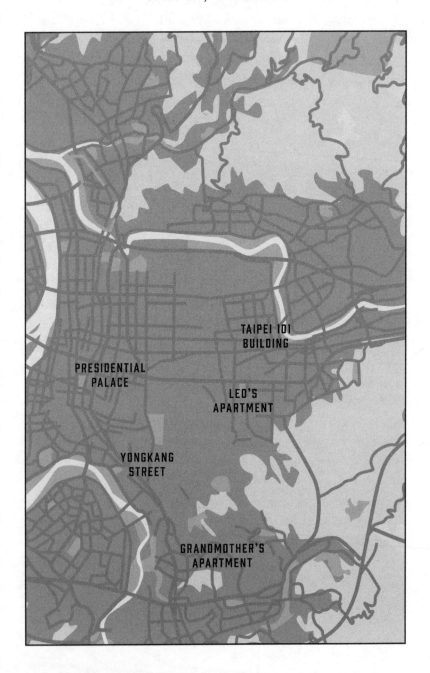

Chapter 14

The Prisoner's Dilemma

There was something deeply chilling in Evelyn Chang's tone, a strange calm, a kind of icy detachment, as if the brutality she had endured had been happening to somebody else. That brutality had not abated, not by a long shot. In the background, I could hear her captors shouting at her, sputtering death threats. From time to time, she'd fall silent, take a sharp breath. In those moments of silence, I would later learn, her captors were pressing a bolo knife against her throat or holding a loaded gun to her head. But even that couldn't break her preternatural calm. I could tell from her voice that somewhere, deep in her wounded psyche, Evelyn had crossed a threshold. She was beyond fear, even beyond pain, and had come to accept the idea that perhaps her tormentors were in fact her salvation, and that her family, her friends, everyone who had been agitating for her release, were her adversaries.

As we'd suspected, Stockholm syndrome was starting to take her.

Nothing in my background had taught me how to break through the wall that she herself was building. Certainly, the military had gone to great lengths to train us to steel ourselves against such things. I'll never forget spending four days of hell in a mock prison camp, just so the Army could prepare me in case I ever was captured, so I'd be able to resist succumbing the way Evelyn was succumbing. But they hadn't taught us how to reach somebody else in the grips of Stockholm syndrome. With increasing desperation, I tried to distill the entire message of all that training into six simple words: "Never forget who the enemy is." My POW resistance training instructors had drummed those words into me years earlier, in the harsh, cold wilderness of western North Carolina at SERE School. The enemy can manipulate and control every aspect of your life during captivity except your will to resist and escape—never stop fighting back in any way that you can and always keep the faith. I tried to match Evelyn's unnatural calm as I repeated those words in Chinese, over and over again: Never forget who the enemy is (不要忘記敵人是誰). *Bu yao wangji diren shi shei. Bu yao wangji diren shi shei.* But I could tell that the words had lost something in translation.

I don't know if she heard me. I don't know if she understood. A sense, deeper than cold dread, more like icy panic, welled up in me, and I realized I had made a terrible mistake. Perhaps a fatal one.

From the moment I had boarded that plane to leave Zamboanga, I had been haunted by the cold, accusatory look in Dennis's and Nick's eyes, and in the eyes of their Scout Rangers. I had vowed that I would prove to them, and maybe to myself, that I had not abandoned them, that I was still very much on the mission.

I had concocted this half-baked plan. After covertly briefing the Chang family, over the phone, on the status of the operation on the ground in the Philippines, I slipped away from my mother's side and made my way to the house of Leo, the poor guy Evelyn had plucked from the fog of her memory when she was first kidnapped, plunging him into the heart of this darkness. His mother's flat was still the nerve center of communications, and I waited there for Abu Sayyaf to call.

I didn't have to wait long. With each passing day, the terrorists were becoming more agitated, more desperate. They called with shocking regularity, and this time, I picked up the phone. It was a spur-of-the-moment decision. In hindsight, it was harebrained, more an impulse than an idea. I thought I could pose as Evelyn Chang's Taiwanese physician, speak only Chinese, and communicate directly with her. I could sense that the terrorists weren't buying it, not for a minute. They angrily, threateningly, demanded that I speak English, but I told Evelyn to insist that I didn't speak English.

I had never spoken to her before, never heard her voice. "I'm a friend," I said, instructing her to speak only in Chinese. I told her that I would help her, that I had spent almost my entire adult life as a professional in this dangerous world, that I had been trained for operations like this. I implored her to trust me as a family friend. She didn't. Instead, she repeated the terrorists' demands and insisted that her family liquidate everything—beg, borrow, and steal if need be—to raise the $3 million, or else, and she said this with a terrifying calm, "They will kill me."

I don't know what I expected to accomplish. I don't know if I intended to stiffen Evelyn's resolve or reassure myself that I was still somehow relevant to her rescue. In either case, I failed. The call quickly devolved into utter chaos, and a brutal chaos at that: screaming and shouting, the sound of blows landing, and then nothing.

Finally, one of the terrorists grabbed the phone. "You're a Taiwan spy!" he screamed. "We'll cut off her head!"

Then the line went dead. My first thought was, *God, what have I done?*

I understood instantly that I had placed Evelyn in even greater jeopardy. In a kidnapping or hostage situation, there is nothing more deadly than silence. Later on, I learned the man who screamed at me was a well-known Abu Sayyaf fighter named Abu Rader.

My thoughts reeled. I grabbed my phone and frantically punched in the numbers I had for Dennis, for Nick, for anyone on the ground in Zamboanga, to explain what I had done. I had no idea how to explain why I'd done it, but I needn't have bothered. Almost before the call with Evelyn ended, their sources in the terrorist camp relayed to them the magnitude of the disaster.

The way they saw it, not only had I put Evelyn in deeper peril, but I also had so alarmed the terrorists that I had now put their sources at risk. I called and called again, but they never took my calls. They had cut me off, abandoned me as they believed I had abandoned them.

I have experienced some colossal failures in my life, and I have made some terrible decisions, both in my military career and in my personal life. Some decisions were made in the spur of the moment, some out of the hubris that comes from being raised in a culture and a family that simply expects that you will always succeed, and some out of fear that those expectations can never be met. But every time, I somehow found the spark that it takes to shake off the numbness and shame and get up off the canvas. I had done it at West Point, I had done it in Ranger training, and I had done it again as a Green Beret in wartime. With the Evelyn Chang case, I had begun to do it again after my career abruptly stopped at Palantir.

But never before had I made so grave an error in judgment. And what made it worse was that this time, it wasn't my future hanging in the balance; it was Evelyn Chang's life. The mission that was to be her salvation had become a smoldering ruin. And it was entirely my fault.

Then, once again, my mother materialized with yet another demand. We had been invited, she told me, to join my grandmother for her weekly dinner with my uncle, but not at my grandmother's modest apartment this time. No, the affairs of state were weighing heavily on my uncle, and this time dinner would be at the presidential palace.

I desperately wanted to say no, to hide from everything and wallow in despair over the crisis I had created. But if I did, then I'd have to explain. I'd have to confess to my mother that I had defied her, that I had blundered into the Evelyn Chang kidnapping case, and that now, because of me, Evelyn's life hung by a thread.

I couldn't face that. At the appointed time, I accompanied my mother and my grandmother through the gates of the presidential palace and into the imposing home of the leader of the nation. It was just us, just family, but still there was a courtly formality to our dinner. I greeted him, calling him Uncle with all the deference and respect that word carries in Chinese culture and more. I might as well have been calling him "Mr. President."

Though he had always loomed large over my family, I barely knew the man. In fact, I didn't know him as a man at all. He was more of an icon than an uncle, a distant figure in my life. Growing up, he might as well have been one of the portraits of long-gone ancestors that graced the tiny shrine at the front door of my grandmother's apartment. I had been raised on stories of his many accomplishments, his Harvard Law School scholarship, his rise to prominence in the fractious world of Taipei politics. But I didn't know him in any real sense of the word. He was barely a real person to me, more like a character out of a fable, silent and austere, a symbol of all that I might achieve if I could only get my act together.

I can't tell you that the stories of his political career inspired me to force my way into West Point. Perhaps they did, and I didn't know it, preferring to credit soldier turned author Gus Lee as my inspiration. I can tell you that my uncle was a major reason why I left the American military. Not because of anything he did. Not because of anything I did. Simply because he was.

After twelve years in the military, after slogging my way through the jungles of the Philippines and the deserts of Iraq, I was selected for an early promotion to major—a significant achievement for a guy who narrowly survived plebe year at West Point—and I was plotting out my next career steps. If I remained in the military, then I was considering heading to another harder, longer Selection and trying out for a secretive, supporting unit to ████████, and I thought I had a shot. After all, I had defied expectations before. I also applied to a few of America's very best graduate schools, which I could consider committing further time to the Army to pay for my education—or I could cover it on my own with the Post-9/11 GI Bill, and see what else the world had to offer. It seemed easiest to stay in the Army after everything I had built up in my career by this point.

While I was cooling my heels in Okinawa, considering my options, a job opportunity came up. The Army was looking for a military attaché in Taiwan for a two-month assignment, and one of my superior officers figured that with my fluent Chinese and my familiarity, such as it was, with Taiwan, I might be a good fit. The idea appealed to me. Mostly because I love Taiwan.

I wanted to make sure that he had all the facts, and so, almost in passing, I mentioned for a second time to my Okinawa unit that my uncle was a famous politician and now the sitting President of Taiwan. I had rarely brought it up before, not because it was a secret—it wasn't— but because the first time I had mentioned it, I was greeted with a roll of the eyes and the vague insinuation that I was name-dropping.

My immediate superior didn't seem at all impressed, nor did he see it as a problem. His bosses did, though. They demanded to know how it was possible that I—a US Army Special Forces officer with a top secret security clearance, as all Green Beret officers are required to have— could have hidden such a critical piece of information from them. The simple fact was that it was not a question that anybody had ever bothered to ask. We were all repeatedly coached to answer security clearance questions as directly and simply as possible to avoid offering any extraneous information that might cause any delays or issues when filling out the lengthy questionnaire process. Loyalty was not a top concern with US Army Special Forces captains who already had voluntarily sacrificed their lives and bodies over the hardest training and highest-risk combat missions America offers. The primary red flags were financial debt and previous drug abuse, neither of which were issues for me. Nevertheless, my superiors demanded that I sit down with an intelligence officer and be questioned immediately and urgently, providing little to no context as to what was happening. It was already the end of the day, but I was brusquely informed that I was not to leave "The Box"—the Okinawa unit headquarters building—under any circumstances in the meantime, as if I posed a flight risk.

I was furious. For nearly half my life, I had worn their uniform, fought their battles, put my life and the lives of my men at risk, and for what? To have my loyalty questioned because of an accident of birth, a blood connection to a man I had never really spoken to and barely knew? Maybe it was just a typical bureaucratic snafu, but I felt that there was an element of a witch hunt to it, the same kind of dull and almost mindless bias that I had felt from time to time at West Point. I entirely understood why the unusual situation should be looked into, which was why I had proactively disclosed it years before. I could not understand the way that I was curtly told, without any explanation, to *immediately* wait for an intelligence officer to interview me as if I were suddenly discovered to be guilty of a heinous crime that urgently needed a sentencing, forcing me to wait for hours past close of business, alone with my thoughts and fears of being forever doubted as a foreigner by the country I had pledged to defend with my life.

It was a thirty-minute interview. Not an interrogation. In fact, the poor intelligence officer who had drawn the short straw repeatedly said that I had done nothing wrong as I answered every question, glowering with malice and indignation.

I knew that, God damn it. But they had stepped on an enormous land mine with me. Accidentally, but that was irrelevant. Anger welled up in me over a lifetime of being seen—or at least believing that I was seen—as someone who was less of an American because of the color of my skin and the cant of my eyes. It was bitter. After twelve years of wearing the flag, after everything I made it through at West Point and beyond, under oath to defend the Constitution, they had questioned my loyalty, my patriotism, my honor without a second thought. Guilty until proven innocent. And I did not believe that I could ever feel safe in the organization after that, no matter how pure my intentions continued to be and no matter that I was immediately cleared of any wrongdoing.

I had already been musing, considering my next moves, at an inflection point as a post-command captain, but I made the decision right then and there that I would leave the military at the end of my hitch within the month. This event shoved me over the line, and while I voluntarily left the military, it festered deeply in my heart and felt like I was being thrown out onto the street—not by the actual Army, nor by my bosses, but by the universe. The moment that my uncle became the President of Taiwan, my career as a US Army Special Forces officer ended, and I just had not realized it yet. I spent the next decade looking over my shoulder, wondering how I'd left the only organization in which I had ever felt like I truly belonged. When the plane took off from Okinawa, I looked out the window at the rolling white waves against the hard reef for the last time and I found myself weeping uncontrollably in front of the other passengers, suddenly overcome by fear and uncertainty. What was I supposed to do with my life now?

My uncle never knew any of this. I certainly never told him. It's not the kind of thing you confide to a stranger.

Our dinner was quiet and cordial. Not warm but pleasant. I studied my uncle from across the table. I was certain that on top of all the grinding pressure of the presidency, the fate of Evelyn Chang weighed heavily on him. It had to. The daily drumbeat of press coverage had slowed but not stopped. He showed no outward sign that she was on his mind. In fact, he never mentioned her name. I suspected that he knew—even if my mother didn't—that I had insinuated myself into the case at Angela Chang's behest. After all, he was the head of state, and Taiwan's intelligence apparatus is not poorly resourced. He presumably had eyes and ears in Leo's apartment, and in Manila, and I imagined that he may already have been fully briefed on the disastrous phone call with the kidnappers that afternoon. If I had been in his shoes, I certainly would have made sure that I knew every development, because that's what a leader must do.

And yet he never said a word about her. But then, just before we left, he guided me toward the spot where our two family mottos—rendered in the same calligraphy as those in my grandmother's home—were framed: Books are treasures, gold is worth nil and All is hollow save works of goodwill. 黃金非寶書為寶。萬事皆空善不空.

Maybe it was just an indulgence by a venerated elder, an empty gesture. But I could not shake the feeling that my uncle was trying to tell me something, or perhaps it was just the universe speaking to me through him. Or, rather, my grandfather speaking his final words of advice to me again through his only son. I felt that something was trying to prod me, in the depths of my despair, to dig a little deeper, to find the strength to do what I needed to do, for Evelyn's sake and for my own.

When I walked into the presidential palace that evening, I did not know what I was going to do next. But I can't help but believe that the universe did. And by the time I left, I did too.

The next morning, I booked a flight to Manila. I'd find Dennis and Nick, and I'd win them back, no matter what it took. I had to. Evelyn Chang's life depended on it. In a way, I suppose, mine did too.

JOLO ISLAND, SULU ARCHIPELAGO

Chapter 15

Pull the Trigger

I didn't hear him coming, didn't see him slip through the sparse lunch crowd at the TGIF back at the Eastwood Mall outside Manila, but when I looked up from my drink, there he was.

"West Pointer to West Pointer?" I asked.

"West Pointer to West Pointer."

It had taken half a dozen unreturned phone calls and every bit of text and email persuasion I could muster to get him there. I had appealed to his sense of military duty, to the war against Abu Sayyaf, but none of that was enough to make Dennis Eclarin forget the fact that, in his eyes, I had abandoned him and his men, wasting his generous charity and time, by walking away from the mission at a crucial moment. The minute I left, they'd just stopped the mission, firing me—and Evelyn—the way they imagined I had fired them. But when I talked again about our factory girl, the extreme danger she was in, he softened and agreed to meet.

Dennis told me that in the time I had been gone, Evelyn's situation had become even more precarious. The Philippine 3rd Marine Brigade, based on Jolo, had received a tip about her whereabouts and had conducted a wide-sweeping operation that had sent Abu Sayyaf scurrying. Evelyn shared later that Sihata Latip and the others frantically woke her up one evening, dragged her through the jungle to the ocean, placed her in a wooden boat, and rowed her out to sea. Once sufficiently far away, they jumped into another boat and left her out there for nearly the entire night, hands and feet bound, staring at the night sky filled with stars.

The moles inside the camp reported the event, and the NICA operatives spent the entire night in rubber Zodiac boats, randomly searching around the southern side of Jolo Island in the pitch-black Sulu Sea, hoping to catch a break. Just before daylight, the Abu Sayyaf members returned to Evelyn's boat and took her back into captivity. Although the Abu Sayyaf subgroup and their side of the Evelyn Chang mission was unaffected, the marine operation had rattled them tremendously.

Additionally, in the wake of my disastrous telephone call, when I had clumsily masqueraded as Evelyn's physician, Abu Sayyaf's usual paranoia had reached a fever pitch in the camp, and it was probably only a matter of days before they'd rid themselves of her, perhaps by selling her off to that one-armed bandit Radullan Sahiron, the top leader of all Abu Sayyaf, and his five hundred men in their impenetrable redoubt deep in the jungles of Patikul's mountains. Sahiron already had sixteen hostages there. He could handle one more, and if he got his one good hand on her, chances were that he'd hold her forever. Or worse, he might not take her at all, and we'd never even find her body.

There was no time to waste, and almost immediately, Dennis and I were once again aboard a puddle jumper nosing its way into the airport in Zamboanga. There wasn't much conversation as we rattled down the shell-shattered pavement and then drove the rocky back roads toward the dilapidated safe house at the edge of the wounded city.

Nick was there to greet us, if you can call the icy stare he gave me a greeting.

Nick was a professional. However strained his feelings about me were, he plunged himself right back into the mission because Dennis, his senior brother, asked him to, and that's all that was required in a filial, hierarchical society like that of the Philippines. And Dennis was helping me because Joe Felter, his senior brother, had asked him to. *Xiaoshun.* I watched with amazement as Nick began negotiating with the terrorists over the phone again. He continued to pose as a local go-between, continuing his existing cover story to Abu Sayyaf as a local engineer whose company supposedly had a Taiwanese connection, not all that different from the role Lady Ann had been expected to play. Nick was born for the role. Literally. He had been raised in the neighborhood and was fluent in all the local dialects, which was why NICA requested him by name on loan from the Scout Rangers, and he proceeded to work on Abu Sayyaf's chief negotiator, a man named Idang Susukan. He knew what buttons to push, and he understood what drove the guys on the other end of the line.

Nick had grown up with some of those who later went on to join Abu Sayyaf, and he knew them as well as he knew himself. He knew their fears, their weaknesses. He knew how to put them at ease, and he knew how to exploit them. On the phone, he altered his voice and his personality to be more local to the area, in effect doing exactly what I had tried to do by posing as Evelyn's doctor. Nick did it so thoroughly and effectively that the terrorists didn't doubt him for a moment.

It was an Academy Award–winning performance, and by the time Nick was done, the terrorists had knocked a zero off their breathtaking demand for $3 million. While they were still demanding far more than we had—far more than the Chang family could afford—it was progress, and for the next several hours, I pulled every string I knew to find somebody who could front us the money. To this day, it remains highly classified as to where the cash came from, but before you could say "Bob's your uncle," Dennis and I had flown to Manila, made our way to a large bank, met surreptitiously with the bank manager in the middle of the night, and were on our way back with a giant satchel full of Philippine pesos. In typical Dennis fashion, he waved his Jedi hands in front of the airport security, and I just stuffed all that cash in a carry-on and put it in an overhead luggage bin on the flight.

The plan was simple, elegant, and dangerous as hell. As we had expected, the terrorists agreed to meet at the home of a highly respected local imam, a man both Abu Sayyaf and Nick knew and deeply trusted. But there was a catch. The Scout Rangers bringing the money and the bomb-making electronics had to show up unarmed. That part was not negotiable. Of course, the Abu Sayyaf members did not know they had been speaking to their mortal enemy Scout Rangers the entire time, and it would take balls of brass to march into a roomful of men you'd been trying to kill for a generation with no way of defending yourself.

The Scout Rangers, to their credit, didn't flinch at the request, even though nobody traveled in Jolo without a weapon. This was a place that still had duels, where the combatants effectively engaged in sword fights—many men carried large machetes or indigenous swords as a primary form of self-defense.

Just in case, though, in addition to their trusty Colt 1911 pistols, they brought three sniper rifles and tucked them away in a satchel. Once the terrorists handed Evelyn over, and she and the NICA operatives were safely out of range, the three Scout Ranger snipers, whose names and involvement remain classified due to current operations, would set up an overwatch position, pick off the terrorists as they made their way back to camp, and retrieve the bomb-making materials and the cash.

The Scout Rangers also had a couple of demands of their own. Not for the terrorists but for me. They would put their lives on the line, I was told. They'd willingly step outside their day-to-day mandate and help with a private kidnap-and-ransom situation, against standing orders. They'd rescue Evelyn Chang, but they required that one of their own lead the sniper ambush and also that I not be allowed to go at all.

In hindsight, I know it was the right call, as it was an officially declared war zone. Even the Scout Rangers and NICA operatives had to request permission to enter the battle space from the Philippine 3rd Marine Brigade, just like I had to when I was in Kurdistan with ODA 121 and wanted to hit targets in Mosul from the conventional infantry.

It was a ridiculous notion that a foreign civilian could be allowed to participate alongside the military in a combat zone. At the time, I was indignant.

I had seen myself at least shadowing the Scout Ranger sniper team leader, as I had done so many times in Iraq, helping him rain hell on the terrorists who had tortured Evelyn Chang. I wanted to get a piece of them myself. I felt I had earned that satisfaction, accustomed as a Green Beret to hit the targets we'd developed. I stormed back to the shack where Dennis and I were bunked, and I seethed as I stared at a crack in the wall. An ant, about the size of your thumb, emerged from the crack. I crushed it. And as soon as I did, another took its place. *There's always another ant to replace the one you just crushed,* I thought to myself. *That's the way it's always been. That's the way it always will be.*

A kind of peace settled over me. It wasn't an epiphany. It wasn't something I had just learned. It was something that I had always known. I just didn't know that I knew it. My job had never been to swing the hammer, nor will it ever be, even now as a CEO. Sure, the Army had spent millions of dollars teaching me to do it, when and if the time came, but that was not why they had schooled me and trained me as a Green Beret. My job was to build a team that would swing the hammer for themselves. That had always been my paramount mission, as it is today. My gun is not my weapon. I am the weapon, and the things I use—hands, feet, knives, guns, tanks, computers—are just tools that make that weapon more lethal and extend the range of its lethality. Perhaps ultimately, my voice is the greatest tool I wield, as it is the primary tool I use to win friends and influence others, as I had done here. A Scout Ranger and a NICA operative team were moving to support my agenda, to risk their lives, and to help my family friend. Just a month before, I had been a complete stranger. I realized how perilously close I had been to failing at that mission when I flew off to Taiwan at my mother's behest, but once again, I had been given a second shot, the latest in a long line of second shots. This was their country and their enemy, not mine. This time, I would listen to others, adjust the windage and elevation, and get the shot on target.

Their second demand was this: no one could know that they had conducted this heroic operation. Regardless of whether it succeeded or failed, they told me, I would have to be the public face of the operation. They should not be doing this sort of thing. I'd take the credit, but I'd also take the heat. I knew that even under the best of circumstances, if everything went exactly as planned, I might be branded as a grandstander, one of the greatest offenses a Green Beret can commit in the eyes of his former comrades, the antithesis of being a "Quiet Professional," one of the other nicknames for US Army Special Forces operators. I hated the idea. But these were some of the most heroic men I had ever met; I didn't have the right to place them in any greater peril than I already had. I was honor bound to agree.

In the heat of the day, Dennis was snoring lightly in his bunk, taking a siesta, one of the few customs the Spanish introduced to the Philippines that Filipinos wholeheartedly embrace. I decided to take a walk. I stumbled around a bit, then dropped in on the slapdash hut that served as the unit's headquarters. I struck up a conversation with Colonel Aldred Limoso, the NICA intelligence operative in command of the Region 9 section of Mindanao and Sulu, and it quickly dawned on me that while we had all been focused on negotiating with the terrorists, virtually no work had been done on the plan for the Scout Ranger attack after Evelyn's rescue. As I had learned in the boxing ring and on the battlefield, always counterattack—the enemy's guard is down after they strike.

I scoured the maps of the terrain where the exchange was to take place, the road back to the camp area, and the camp area itself. I sent for transparent overlays and colored pens, and I went old-school as I scoured the broad landscape for hidden risks, for places that would provide cover for an ambush, employing a careful terrain-analysis process that we spent weeks and all-nighters perfecting at the six-month Infantry Officers Advanced Course for rising captains at Fort Benning.

In particular, I spent time mapping and identifying the natural exfiltration routes out of the Abu Sayyaf camp, sussing out spots where they might stop to regroup. I went through this process as much for the sake of killing time as to provide potentially useful information for the Scout Rangers.

We were working with one hand tied behind our back. In an American-run operation, we could count on air cover and state-of-the-art artillery to soften up our adversary before we faced them head-on, but there was none of that in this godforsaken place. All we had at our disposal were three poorly maintained mobile 105mm howitzers with a theoretical kill range of twenty yards, assuming they fired correctly, plus a few mortars. In fact, the howitzers were the exact same antiques that we'd used in Operation Ultimatum, still sitting on top of the Bud Dajo hilltop in the middle of Jolo Island. I sketched out a general templated plan to stage three quick barrages, first with the howitzers; then, after a long delay, the 60mm light-infantry mortars could get close enough to allow our Scout Rangers to use the confusion as cover and sneak in close enough to finish off the terrorists, in hand-to-hand combat if need be. It was the best we could do with what we had.

In jungle warfare, in the chaotic morass of trees and roots and shadows, it's often necessary to slip into knife-fighting range to kill your enemy. This classic light-infantry tactic is called a rolling assault: close in on your enemies by softening and fixing them with indirect fire, until you're close enough that you can hear them, and then, to use the military terminology, close with the enemy and clear the objective. The task here in conventional light-infantry warfare was to destroy, not to disrupt or capture, and words have meaning. Keep pursuing until every single last one of them is dead. Scout Rangers usually operate in small seven-man teams, a hard lesson learned over decades of jungle warfare, and it was rare to conduct a company-level rolling-assault style of raid.

As I was replaying the analysis in my head, I chanced upon another foreigner, an Australian intelligence operative, who was visiting that day and meeting with Nick at one of the bamboo huts on the compound.

The Aussie had nothing to do with our operation, but he had been assigned to monitor and track a bomb-making operation potentially linked to Jemaah Islamiyah, an even more deadly Al-Qaeda offshoot based in Indonesia. Jemaah Islamiyah had been behind a deadly bombing in 2002 that killed 202 people in Bali, including eighty-eight Australians. The group had then bombed the Australian embassy in Jakarta in 2004, killing four more Australians, then slaughtered another four Australians the following year and three more the year after that, when they bombed the J. W. Marriott and the Ritz-Carlton Hotel. The powers that be in the Australian capital of Canberra wanted them stopped, and my newfound friend at the bamboo hut was part of the tip of the spear for that effort.

We chatted for a while, swapping war stories, one Western operative to another, and at some point, we persuaded him to lend us some of the equipment that the Australian taxpayers had been kind enough to provide him with: tiny technical surveillance tracking devices that we could insert into the electronics we were going to provide to Abu Sayyaf. The Australian was a counterpart to Nick, so he was happy to pass the materials over. I don't remember whether I promised to give them back when the operation was over, but I was growing increasingly confident that maybe, just maybe, I would be able to do that. At least we had a plan.

Mike Tyson once said that "everybody has a plan until they get punched in the mouth." You have no idea how true that is.

On the day of the exchange, before first light, the men who would conduct the operation—Limoso himself, Major Manuel "Nick" Juter Gemao, another brave NICA operative still currently in operation code-named ▮▮▮▮▮▮▮▮▮▮ and three other Scout Ranger snipers who would pretend to be civilians and strut, unarmed, into the teeth of Abu Sayyaf—plus the others who would try to finish off the terrorists when the deal was done and they were summoned together and given one last chance to back out. The brass in Manila had somehow gotten word that an operation to rescue Evelyn Chang was imminent, and they had ordered every military asset in the area—helicopters, gunboats, and standby units who could step in if there was trouble—to stand down. If the Scout Rangers and NICA operatives conducted this operation, they wouldn't just be doing it without the official sanction of their government; they would be doing it utterly alone and in direct defiance of an implied order from the presidential office at Malacañang Palace. They'd be putting their careers on the line, risking court-martial and imprisonment, as well as their lives. That was doubly more than anyone could reasonably expect of them. They were told that there would be no shame attached to anyone who, even at that late moment, decided to back out.

Not one of them did. To a man, they volunteered, ready to lay down their lives to save a stranger. The objective might have been the rescue of an innocent woman whom none of them had ever heard of before being swept up into this operation, but this was bigger than one woman's life. This was their fight. This was their calling. Regardless of what their leadership in Manila thought.

I'm not ashamed to say that I choked up a little when I saw that.

Whenever I think back on this story, I remember that there is no light without the darkness, and the night is darkest before the dawn. This is the backdrop to the horrors of war and poverty, where we see humankind's greatest attributes: loyalty, honor, and sacrifice. While the history of the Philippines contains dark elements—remote, poverty-stricken areas, the lawless kidnapping of foreigners from neighboring countries—it also has its heroes, like the Scout Rangers and the NICA operatives who put themselves at risk to save a complete stranger. Friendship comes in many forms, does it not?

We watched from a distance, electronically, as Gemao, ███████, and the three Scout Ranger snipers made their way to the imam's house. Separately, Limoso went to the Philippine 3rd Marine Brigade headquarters, as planned under the cover story of gaining access into the battle space for inspecting a NICA facility on the base. When he arrived, he leaned on the marine colonel, his Philippine Military Academy classmate, the country's equivalent of West Point, to cease all military operations until further notice. This was an enormous request for a brigade-size element, but it was a requirement from Abu Sayyaf to conduct the exchange, due to the previous scare. While surprised and irritated at being fooled originally, the marine colonel agreed for the sake of their friendship, despite being kept in the dark on the rogue operation.

Back at the imam's house, two Scout Ranger snipers stayed outside, providing coverage, while Gemao, ███████, and a third sniper went inside. The place was three stories high, a testament to the imam's standing in the region. On the first floor was a veritable arsenal where rocket-propelled grenades (RPGs) and hand grenades and heavy machine guns, AK-47s and M16s, were stored, a reminder of just how volatile a flock this shepherd tended—praise the Lord and pass the ammunition.

If they were frightened, as anyone in their right mind would be, they showed no sign of it. Gemao and ███████ made their way to the imam's spacious second-floor sitting room, where they waited while the third Scout Ranger sniper went upstairs to the rooftop to secretly safeguard the money and electronics, and to find a good position to hit the Abu Sayyaf members on the way out to recover the materials. The other two Scout Ranger snipers had a clear shot to protect Gemao and ███████ through the large glass windows surrounding the second floor.

As soon as two young terrorists arrived, the plan took a potentially lethal turn. Evelyn was not with them, and the Abu Sayyaf envoys, in coarse, crude barks, announced that the exchange was going to take place elsewhere, at a location of their choosing. As the primary negotiator, Gemao would go alone, while ███████ remained behind as insurance, under the watch of these two teenage terrorists, who, while they waited, would amuse themselves with a friendly game of catch using hand grenades they had brought. Anything funny happens, they said to ███████, we pull the pins, and we all go together to meet Allah.

Soon enough, eight more terrorists would arrive, ringing the house and isolating ███████, with three hidden Scout Ranger snipers in support.

You can imagine what must have been going through their minds. Here they were, going rogue by operating against orders, with no government backup, in the hands of Abu Sayyaf, with a satchel full of cash and a bagful of potential IED equipment. What was to stop the terrorists from simply taking the cash and devices, and then holding the Scout Rangers and NICA operatives hostage and demanding more ransom or, worse, just killing them? The risk would be even greater if the terrorists figured out that these brave men were not merely engineers from the local construction company but Abu Sayyaf's sworn enemies: the fearsome Scout Rangers and the cunning NICA operatives.

I've never been a prisoner, never had my fate so thoroughly in someone else's hands, and I can only begin to imagine the thoughts that must have been going through their minds.

Thinking back on it later put me in mind of a training exercise I had done in South Korea with my most cherished and influential Green Beret mentor, Tony Bell, as part of my preparation for the US Army Combat Diver Qualification Course, referred to colloquially as "Scuba School," one of the most physically demanding courses in the US Army Special Forces, held in Key West, Florida. I never was able to secure a school slot in the end, but I was indelibly influenced by one of the key challenges, called "drown-proofing"—during "Pre-Scuba," a required hell week to qualify for a school slot—which required the epitome of mental discipline in order to be truly comfortable in open water. In the simulation we were blindfolded, bound hand and foot, and thrown into ten feet of water. We had been told that our only chance of survival was to allow ourselves to sink to the bottom and then push off with all our might, break the surface, gasp for a breath, and sink to the bottom again. And then do it again, and again and again. For how long? In real life, until you drowned or were rescued. For the course, it was five minutes. It seemed ridiculous to me at the time, but now I understand it. The exercise was never meant to teach survival. It was an exercise in learning how to believe that in the absolute worst of circumstances, you had the faith that you could survive on your own.

Lesser men might have panicked at the sudden turn of events and resisted, and the results would likely have been disastrous, certainly for them and almost certainly for Evelyn. Nick got on the phone with Idang Susukan, and the two men engaged in a final battle of wits. In the end, the Scout Ranger and the NICA operative remained calm and did as they were told. It was an act of tremendous courage, and more than that, it was a remarkable profession of faith in their fellow Scout Rangers—and a commitment to the last line of the US Army and the Armed Forces of the Philippines' Scout Ranger Creed, a shared creed word for word, indicative of the deep military ties between the two countries—"to fight on to the Ranger objective and complete the mission though I be the lone survivor." Literally. This was about mission completion, and Rangers never stop until the job is done.

As soon as he heard about the change in plans, Limoso hurtled out of his command-and-control room at the Philippine 3rd Marine Brigade headquarters, corralled a jeepney (a colorful Mazda Bongo truck), grabbed a local-based NICA operative ████████████████████ as his driver, and ordered him to follow the dirt road deep into Abu Sayyaf territory. Limoso worried that Gemao would be out of communication and set up a relay point between Gemao and ████████ to coordinate for the exchange, entirely exposed and vulnerable. They were risking their own lives for Evelyn Chang, a stranger, and their comrades. Leave no man behind.

It seemed to take an eternity to make it to the camp in southern Maimbung. This was the same terrain I had briefly visited as a battle captain when my first Special Forces team, ODA 121, was based there with a Philippine infantry battalion during Operation Ultimatum, the kind of terrain you imagine when you hear the word "jungle," a place where you could imagine all kinds of predators, human and animal, watching your every move in the thick undergrowth, peering at you from the tall elephant grass.

When Gemao finally made it to the meeting point, eighteen Abu Sayyaf terrorists were there, including the "big boss," Sihata Latip, the first time any friendly element had ever seen his face. Both Evelyn and Nick told me that Sihata Latip was cleanly bald, with a very long and frizzy beard and an intensely angry face. Gemao remembered that the Colt 1911 he had hidden in his pocket, that weapon first developed to kill the ancestors of these Moros, held ten rounds. He swore to himself that he would take the big boss with him, if he had been fooled into this Abu Sayyaf camp all along, and they would die together then and there.

He was still calculating the odds against him ever making it out alive when suddenly, Evelyn appeared, escorted by another group of Abu Sayyaf terrorists, led by none other than one of the other top leaders and the chief negotiator for Evelyn's life—Idang Susukan. As with Sihata Latip, it was the first time anybody outside Abu Sayyaf had seen his face. Gemao would remember it for many years to come.

As soon as he had her, he sent out the code word—ARROW— instructing ▓▓▓▓▓▓▓ to release the ransom money and the electronics with the tracking device to the Abu Sayyaf envoys back at the imam's house. Once the ten Abu Sayyaf fighters began departing, the three Scout Ranger snipers begged to take the clear shots and recover the money and electronics, but Gemao declined, respecting the imam's impartial guarantee of safety—honor aside, this ended up being a critically strategic and fortuitous decision.

"See you later, Nick the Engineer," Sihata Latip said ominously as Gemao and Evelyn climbed into their truck and sped off.

Evelyn was in shock. I suppose the terrorists were too. Gemao, Adil (the driver), and Evelyn headed off as fast as they could on those treacherous roads to link up with Limoso's jeepney halfway, then toward the Philippine 3rd Marine Brigade camp a few miles away, next to Camp Bautista, where I had lived and operated for six months during Operation Ultimatum. Evelyn was out. But she still was not free, and she still was not safe.

They made it only a few miles before being ambushed, and they began to dodge sporadic gunfire. To this day it remains unclear whether Abu Sayyaf launched the ambush or if it was one of the many renegade bands of bandits or violent indigenous tribes who prowl those jungles prosecuting endless clan disputes. The two drivers pressed the pedal to the metal in a harrowing and panicked ride, and the getaway vehicle hurtled violently on the bumpy jungle roads, throwing the passengers about.

Even after they had run that gauntlet, they still were not out of harm's way. Ancient lines of communication in these jungles are often faster and more efficient than modern cell and satellite phones, and news of Evelyn and the rogue element's escape was out before they were halfway to the marine camp on Jolo. Those same lines of communication had also urgently informed us that Malaysian special-branch intelligence operatives were on our heels.

Maybe they just wanted to pat us on the back, say "attaboy," and swap a few stories about Abu Sayyaf, maybe get together and sing a karaoke version of "We Are the Champions" to celebrate Evelyn's rescue. But nothing in the intelligence I had heard up to that point made me think so. We worried that—desperate to burnish their reputation after the embarrassment of having a foreigner snatched from one of their resorts, resulting in a regionally headlining news story—they might have been plotting to take Evelyn from the Scout Rangers before she could leave the Philippines, likely on her way to the airport in Zamboanga. We thought perhaps they would want to spirit her back to Pom Pom Island and claim she had never left Malaysia and the authorities recovered her safely. We didn't know. We had no official cover. That made us even more vulnerable. We were on edge, and our minds and emotions were all over the place.

The NICA operatives, appreciating the danger, had armed themselves and quietly handed me a gun as well, another violation of local conventions, since foreigners are prohibited from carrying guns in the Philippines. Under the circumstances, they decided it was a rule best observed in the breach.

If the bullets started flying, they wanted another shooter on their side, and frankly, if the situation turned bleak, I still trusted myself over anybody else to return effective fire, as any self-respecting Green Beret would. And so there we were, armed to the teeth, assuming that the Malaysians were as well. We were prepared—as prepared as we could be—for the worst. But we were hoping for the best. The last thing we wanted was a fight, especially with Evelyn in tow, and there was no way I was going to let her be snatched away a second time.

It was a tense few miles on the way back to the marine base, and the Scout Rangers and NICA operatives did not know what to expect when they got there. After all, they were on what amounted to a rogue mission to rescue one stranger at the behest of another who had no official ties whatsoever to the Philippine government, or any government for that matter. The ranking Philippine marine colonel at the base hadn't become a ranking officer by being a fool. He immediately realized that he had been handed a public relations coup. As a matter of fact, Limoso had encouraged him to exploit the angle, judging that doing so would throw anybody who might be trying to sniff out a connection between the rogue operatives and Evelyn's rescue off the scent.

The marine colonel notified the press in Manila and welcomed Evelyn with ostentatiously open arms. He had her poked and prodded by camp physicians, who declared her in surprisingly good health, considering her preexisting medical condition, her broken wrist, and the ordeal she had endured. He had every moment of it preserved on video for posterity, and for the voracious press. At this moment, he accidentally let Evelyn know that Eric Hsu was indeed dead, which is why she is weeping uncontrollably in the videos, having willfully believed he might still be alive until that moment. The marine colonel knew damned well that the same brass in Manila, who just hours earlier had opposed the mission, would now claim credit for its success. To be fair, that impulse is not unique to the Philippines. Such things happen in every military and have for all of recorded history. History is written by the winners, after all, or at least by those smart enough to stand really close to the winners when the cameras start recording.

Within minutes of her arrival, with the quiet approval of the officers in the capital, the marine colonel had arranged to have Evelyn flown out the next morning on the first Evergreen helicopter to Zamboanga, where she would be delivered into the waiting arms of a media already in a frenzy and then taken under custody by our friends at the Anti-Kidnapping Group. As I mentioned earlier, the AKG had not exactly won the undying trust of the Scout Rangers, and I was not taking any chances right at the finish line. My father always taught me that you're only halfway done at the finish line. Stay focused, don't get lax, and finish strong—always finish strong. It's not about how you started, or even how it went along the way. It's about how you close.

Dennis and I understood that while we had succeeded in delivering Evelyn from her captors, we now had an equally complicated task: rescuing her from her newfound friends. We had to spirit her out of a country where I could be accused of having conspired to manipulate an elite military unit into ignoring the wishes of its commanding generals, technically done an end run around official law enforcement authorities, and undermined an official international and domestic police investigation. I had done it all with no legal authority as a foreign civilian or any coverage from my home country. At that point, Evelyn was at risk, but in some ways I felt at greater risk, as I did not know how anybody was going to react to what had just happened. Under cover of night, we smuggled her out of the marine base and loaded her onto a civilian ferryboat that struggled for six hours in the early-morning hours across the sea to Zamboanga, where I would board a plane with her to Manila and then onward to Taipei.

Dennis and I were waiting on the Zamboanga dock when she arrived right at first light. Her Scout Ranger and NICA operative rescuers danced a little jig on the dock when they landed. Evelyn did not. It was the first time I had ever seen her in person, this woman who had been the entire focus of my life for the last thirty-five days. Regardless of what the camp physicians determined, I thought she looked fragile and frightened. The time would come when she would be able to process all that had happened to her, but that time was not yet. She clung to me, and I tried to comfort and reassure her.

I don't know who he spoke to, but Dennis had arranged to have us enter the airport grounds from a side entrance, far from the clutch of journalists, gawkers, and those who might try to sabotage Evelyn's escape for their own sordid reasons. In fact, everybody thought that Evelyn was arriving on the helicopter much later that morning from Jolo, unaware that we had slipped her out overnight on the ferry. We drove almost all the way to the steps of the plane and, shielded from the eyes of the curious and the nefarious, snuck her aboard and headed to Manila.

Dennis texted me that the AKG, the Malaysians, and the media were all stunned when the helicopter landed in Zamboanga, and Evelyn was nowhere to be found. "Ha ha," he texted me while I sat on the runway at Ninoy Aquino International Airport with Evelyn firmly by my side. It seemed like forever before the plane took off, and when at last it did, I glanced out the window and flipped the bird with the Sulu Archipelago in mind. I believed I would never again return to this forgotten corner pocket of the world, though in years to come, I would find myself, with Blackpanda, again entangled with warlords and violent indigenous chieftains over gold mines and copper deposits.

Meanwhile, while we were in the air, a company of sixty Scout Rangers from 1st Battalion back on Jolo immediately began what would be the first of several assaults over the next few months on the Abu Sayyaf subgroup who had kidnapped Evelyn Chang. With the tracking device from our Australian friends, which was both a tracker and a logger, we gathered Idang Susukan's precise movements for three weeks. In the primary raid against the camp where Evelyn was held, they used the same style of classic rolling-assault tactics I had sketched out with the colonel in Zamboanga, and the ground rumbled with the percussion of howitzers, then mortars, then automatic weaponry. Not only that but the Scout Rangers were able to continue attacking Abu Sayyaf in their home jungle, even after they'd broken contact and escaped after each successive raid, due to the ability of the tracker to show exactly where they would likely have retreated.

When the dust settled, the Scout Rangers had destroyed the eighty-person Abu Sayyaf fighter subgroup who'd kidnapped Evelyn Chang led by Yasser Igasan, Idang Susukan, and Sihata Latip.

One of the Abu Sayyaf envoys playing catch with a hand grenade at the imam's house underestimated ██████████ during the tense hours while they waited on the second floor, and he arrogantly exposed his identity as Abu Kaiser, a violent teenager whom ██████████ had been tracking for years as a research analyst prior to volunteering on the spot for the rogue Evelyn Chang mission as a formally untrained operative, Jack Ryan–style. Abu Kaiser demanded that ██████████ hand over his Casio watch, North Face backpack, and New York Yankees ball cap, just a young kid who loved branded merchandise. Spotting an opportunity, as nobody had ever seen the high school–age terrorist's face before, ██████████ offered to send real Levi's jeans to Abu Kaiser, and he gave him a fake LBC number, the Philippine equivalent of FedEx, to pick up at the local Jolo Town LBC office the next day. Abu Kaiser eagerly showed up the next day to collect, and in broad daylight on the street in front of the townspeople, Philippine intelligence operatives gunned him down on sight.

Sihata Latip, the day-to-day Abu Sayyaf lieutenant and Evelyn Chang's "big boss," was killed days later by the Light Reaction Regiment, the Philippine equivalent of ██████████, trained and stood up by the ██, in a kill mission at his home in northern Maimbung, in a spectacular firefight under the cover of darkness and a textbook special forces raid with the latest night-vision goggles and equipment provided by the Green Berets. Apparently, the villagers and family of Sihata Latip were tipped and it was a pitched battle before finally capitulating. They had used our tracking device to find him, vectored in by Nick himself. "See you later, Nick the Engineer," indeed.

Idang Susukan, an even higher-ranking Abu Sayyaf leader and the chief negotiator for Evelyn Chang's life, was wounded in the major Scout Ranger company-size rolling-assault raid at the main camp a month later, with six Abu Sayyaf killed in action and over thirty wounded, that resulted in the need to amputate his arm due to lack of modern medical support. He survived for years after joining his buddy Radullan Sahiron's one-armed status, until suddenly a Philippine military unit claimed they'd killed him in battle and presented enough evidence to claim the dead-or-alive cash reward. And then, in December 2022, the famous Moro leader Nur Misuari traveled to Davao City for negotiations with the Philippine government and guaranteed the safety of a fellow Muslim traveler to stay at his house there. When a real-time photo was shared of the two travelers, Nick, as the only man alive outside Abu Sayyaf who had ever seen Idang Susukan, quickly identified the terrorist, who was detained upon arrival in Davao and confessed his identity. He was killed shortly afterward under custody in prison. If Idang Susukan had never shown his face by bringing Evelyn Chang for exchange, miscalculating that a Taiwanese factory girl could ever have friends like these, he may have operated with impunity for many years to come.

The full details of the impact of the Evelyn Chang tracking-and-logging device for the Scout Rangers and NICA operations against Abu Sayyaf will not be formally declassified until 2032. Until then, suffice it to say that a significant number of terrorists have met their untimely demise, in no small part because of the things that were set in motion during the mission to rescue Evelyn Chang. I have heard rumors from friends at the US Embassy in Manila that their NICA counterparts thought the Americans were the ones secretly feeding them the real-time tactical intelligence on the Abu Sayyaf subgroup's whereabouts, responding with a knowing wink and a nod in the hallways when the

US Embassy confusedly denied any knowledge. They weren't wrong—I am an American.

The last one was especially gratifying to me. Yasser Igasan, one of the top-five adversaries from my Green Beret days in Jolo, had also been seriously wounded in an ensuing Scout Ranger operation in northern Maimbung, at his home close to a holy mountain that members of Abu Sayyaf worshipped. He, too, had been located using the tracking device's intelligence when Idang Susukan visited him, and I like to think that his wounds slowed him down enough that a few years later, the authorities were finally able to kill him. And I like to think that I had something to do with that, that I helped finish a bit more of the job we had begun years earlier in Operation Ultimatum, just like how we wounded Khadaffy Janjalani, the leader of Abu Sayyaf at the time.

The computer electronics we had handed over along with Evelyn's ransom were never used for bomb making. I was relieved, as I could not stand the thought that I had actually increased the enemy's combat power after spending so many years conditioned to destroy them. Indeed, rather than being used to kill civilians or Filipino or American troops, those devices were turned on them, a Trojan horse of sorts. There was something poetic about that. The US$300,000, though, was lost in the fog of war. These things happen. That corner of the Philippines is spiderwebbed with cracks. Sometimes things crawl out of them, and sometimes things fall into them. I think about it now simply as the price we paid for their heads.

Evelyn had escaped Abu Sayyaf, and together we had eluded the many others who had tried to block our way, but there was no escaping the press in Taipei. The moment we landed, we walked into a cyclone of frantic reporters, cameras, and microphones, some of the reporters nearly knocking each other over as they lunged at us. During his address to the media, Richard Chang, Evelyn's older brother, turned to shake my hand in gratitude, and the media took that as a signal to turn their attention toward me. It's a weakness of the media everywhere that stories must be simple, that there are preordained heroes and traditional villains, and one must fit neatly into one category or another. In this case, I was their hero. In their simple narrative, I—the West Pointer, former Green Beret, nephew of the sitting President of Taiwan—had almost single-handedly engineered and executed the rescue of Evelyn Chang, restoring Taiwan's damaged national honor. They needed a hero, and I was a convenient fall guy.

Besides, I had promised the NICA operatives that I would do it. And so I did.

Nothing in the coverage considered how twisted and complicated the road to Evelyn's rescue had been. Nobody knew that I had my own doubts along the way, the mistakes I had made, the nearly tragic errors in judgment that had put Evelyn in greater danger. Not a single reporter knew about what I had learned, about myself, about what it really means to me to have had the honor of serving as a Green Beret. The real story of Evelyn Chang's rescue is about a few villains and a lot of heroes, and my role was to find and to help those heroes become all they could be.

The front pages of the newspapers would never consider any of that. Sooner or later, I knew, I would get a chance to set the record straight. But that day, I had something else on my mind. Evelyn Chang had survived her most perilous ordeal, and it was time for me to face mine. I had to explain what I had been doing to my mother.

BLACKPANDA GROUP

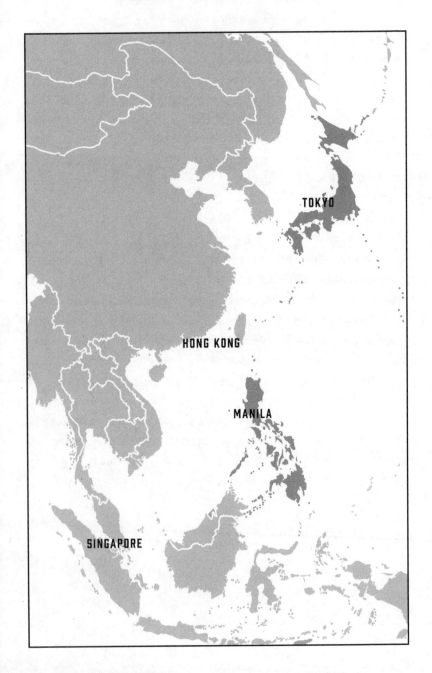

Chapter 16

Redemption Song

It would be comforting to imagine that Evelyn Chang's captivity ended after those tense and fateful thirty-five days in the grip of Abu Sayyaf. It would be reassuring to believe that once she was freed by our efforts, by the heroic actions of the Scout Rangers and NICA operatives, the factory girl's ordeal was over. It would be comforting, indeed. And it would be incorrect. The truth is that it takes a very long time to escape the aftershocks of a trauma like that, and peace comes slowly, if it ever comes. In the years since her rescue, I have watched Evelyn Chang from a distance, and I have come to respect, deeply, the courage and strength she has shown while building back a life that had been so brutally interrupted.

I now realize that the Evelyn Chang case permanently altered the trajectory of my own life. It made me come to understand the meaning of the ancient family mottos that hang in what had been my grandmother's humble flat in Taipei. My grandmother passed away not long after the rescue, and when my uncle's term as President ended, he moved back into the modest family flat. But more than that, the case made me come to appreciate again what it means to be my own man—what I can do and what I am capable of when I put my mind to something—and it opened for me a path that I am pursuing to this day through my company, Blackpanda.

It was not a sudden epiphany by any stretch of the imagination. In fact, in the days immediately following the rescue, my only thought was trying to find a way back to the life I had once had. I signed on with a tech start-up in Singapore, with no goal other than to return to the path I had lost before the Evelyn Chang case began. The way I saw it, I was still getting up from that sidewalk in Hong Kong where my part in the saga began, collecting my possessions, dusting myself off, and moving on.

Of course, I was aware that in the meantime, I had become a minor celebrity in this part of Asia, that a media desperate for a lone hero had been all too willing to anoint me to serve in that role, a guy in camo who had rescued not only a hostage but Taiwan's national honor. I assumed that my promise to the NICA operatives would become less onerous over time and that, with its notoriously short attention span, the media would quickly move on, and I could slip into a kind of comforting anonymity.

I was wrong. I had become the face of the rescue, and in the following weeks and months, I was stalked by the paparazzi, deluged with requests for interviews, and inundated with invitations to give lucrative talks to various gatherings of influential people. At one such event, I was invited to speak at the Republic of China Marine Corps (ROCMC) headquarters in Zuoying, southern Taiwan, for six hours, with ten-minute breaks on the hour. To this day I remain amazed by the fact that I grew bored long before the poor audience did.

It took a while to dawn on me that as a result of my part in the Evelyn Chang rescue, I had been given both an awesome opportunity and a serious responsibility. My old mentor and friend, Matt Pecot, the former Green Beret who had first hired me at Credit Suisse, brought it all into focus for me. He had hit on an idea to establish a company to provide security and advice to governments and industry in the region. He planned to call it Blackpanda, and he approached me with the idea of serving as the CEO and public face of the organization. A very successful senior investment banker in his own right, Matt invested $1 million in the venture. With his record of success in business and the military, I couldn't say no. I was slowly coming to terms with the notion that maybe I could find a way to translate my surprisingly durable fame into something that wouldn't just be financially rewarding, but personally rewarding as well.

And just like that, I was a CEO. Even if it was only on a business card, requiring me to nod graciously as polite elders congratulated my success at the tender age of thirty-five, I scoffed at the legitimacy of the title, given that we'd simply made it up. It took me years, many, many more failures, and a few startling successes to become truly confident enough to call myself a chief executive.

The military had trained me to be a leader, yes. My time in the Philippines and Iraq had made me appreciate that training, but it was the thirty-five days I spent working to free Evelyn Chang that made it all real to me, and the lessons I learned during that operation, often the hard way, have come into play time and again during my years at the helm of Blackpanda.

Not long after that, in 2017, we made an international name for ourselves after a horrific attack at the Resorts World hotel and casino in Manila that killed thirty-seven people. We provided not only the initial response but also an elaborate cybersecurity plan to protect the operation from both terrorists and the shadowy characters on the internet who would exploit that atrocity, which has led us to our current incarnation as the premier cybersecurity incident response company in Asia.

Today we are a leading venture-backed cybersecurity start-up in Asia, having raised over US$23 million to date, and it all began with Evelyn Chang and the notoriety in this part of the world that this event gave me.

They say that we—that I—saved Evelyn Chang. But she also saved me, renewing my confidence that I can change things for the better, using nothing more than my raw ability to solve problems and influence others. Evelyn Chang reminded me of my values, and she reminded me of my value.

Even now, as I write this, it still pains me to talk openly about my accomplishments, for fear that I'll violate the spirit of humility so prized in the family and culture I was raised in as well as the Green Berets and its identity as the "Quiet Professionals." It also pains me to talk about my failures. That, too, is an Asian American trait. It's important that I do both. It's important to every young Asian kid in America, struggling to fit into a culture that sees him as an outsider, no matter how he sees himself. It's important to every Asian kid who's suffocating in a world that often seems to care more about its traditions than his dreams. This book is Evelyn's story, it's the Scout Rangers' and NICA operatives' story, and it's my story. But it's also those kids' story too. I can show them that they can be whatever they choose to be, as long as they can find the courage to get up off the canvas, as I did, time and time again. As the Japanese say, fall down seven times, get up eight.

Most of all, the value I gained from the Evelyn Chang incident was the inspiration from the NICA operatives and Scout Rangers. I realized in that moment that the brotherhood, the camaraderie, and special friendships could never be taken away from me, and that I was part of a special tribe for the rest of my life. They gave me the clarity to simply accept it all as a single, individual component of my journey. They gave me the peace to move on and be entirely something else now.

When I was a kid, my father often quoted a Confucian proverb. At twenty years of age, we're at the apex of our physical power and just peeking out at the very beginning of adulthood. At thirty, we become yoked to our responsibilities, our careers, and the family we may have begun. At fifty, we come to understand the contours of our lives and how the rest of our lives will be until we die. At sixty, we cease to care what the world thinks of us. And at seventy, we become mystical dragons at the twilight of the journey of our lives.

Perhaps the greatest miracle occurs at forty, he says, when we are simply no longer confused about our own identities or our roles in the world. I have to agree. I love the simplicity of this maxim. I love the truth in it. After a long and strange journey—experiencing the confusion and chaos of military combat in Iraq and the Philippines, testing the absolute limits of my strength and resolve, finding resources in myself and others that I hadn't expected during the Evelyn Chang case, and launching Blackpanda—I can now state simply and honestly that I am no longer confused. And I have Evelyn Chang to thank for it.

PHILIPPINES

Epilogue

Their Names Shall Be Remembered

Dennis Eclarin, Aldred Limoso, Manuel "Nick" Juter Gemao, and many more courageous soldiers were never formally acknowledged by their own government, despite putting their lives and careers in jeopardy to rescue a stranger at the request of a man (me) whom they barely knew. Because of the rogue nature of the operation, even the Scout Rangers and NICA do not formally know the full events. Perhaps I do not even know. But a few months after the rescue, they were summoned to the pseudo-Taiwanese consulate in Manila, where the government of the Republic of China, at my urging and petitioning, quietly awarded them the Order of Loyalty and Valor, the first awarded since World War II. Nick, serving as the 2nd Scout Ranger Battalion commander, proudly wears his today on his uniform. Dennis and Aldred are retired, and I like to think they keep them in their offices as a reminder of the time we ran together.

It's been said that a man in his time plays many parts: hero, villain, avenger, victim. No one is one thing forever, and no one knows that better than I do. But on that day, and in my mind forever afterward, these men were heroes. Scout Rangers lead the way.

The straightforward language of the official Taiwanese government citation for the awards can never do justice to the courage and character that these men showed that day. With a few minor errors, it reads, in part:

> On the evening of 20 December, COL Limoso and MAJ Gemao, along with three other NICA operatives and Philippine Army Scout Rangers, boarded a ferry from Zamboanga to Jolo Port, and sailed all night to arrive into Jolo in the early morning hours of 21 December. COL Limoso moved to 3rd Marine Philippine base and pretended to be in Jolo for inspecting a NICA facility to provide cover for MAJ Gemao, who was moving forward to conduct hostage and ransom exchange for Chang An-Wei [Evelyn Chang].

> Just after the ransom payment was counted by [an] Abu Sayyaf courier, the Abu Sayyaf leadership changed their demands and instructed MAJ Gemao to travel alone from Jolo Town (north of Jolo Island, where the planned exchange was to take place) approximately forty-five minutes south by vehicle to the township of Maimbung in Talipao barangay [village], to pick up Evelyn. With the risk of ambush and the added risk and threat that the Abu Sayyaf discovered MAJ Gemao's true identity as a NICA operative, this request was extremely dangerous. With little regard for life and safety, COL Limoso volunteered to travel with MAJ Gemao to Maimbung, upon which they safely retrieved Chang An-Wei out of the guerrilla village, while surrounded by over seventy Abu Sayyaf fighters.

> Upon reaching safely back at the 3rd Philippine Marine base, COL Limoso and MAJ Gemao cleverly tricked

the Philippine Marines that they would be transporting Chang An-Wei via helicopter back to Zamboanga in the morning. Via their intelligence network reporting, COL Limoso and MAJ Gemao discovered that both Malaysian intelligence operatives and corrupt Philippine National Police Anti-Kidnapping Group agents were planning on independently interdicting COL Limoso and MAJ Gemao and taking control of Chang An-Wei, as they were acting illegally. It is unknown if violent action was planned, but it is highly likely as COL Limoso and MAJ Gemao and their rogue team were armed and dangerous. Again, with little regard for safety and their careers, COL Limoso and MAJ Gemao snuck out of the Marine base with Chang An-Wei late that night, clandestinely traveling via civilian ferry to Zamboanga Port. [We] received them at approximately 6 am at Zamboanga on 21 December, and we safely moved Chang An-Wei without incident through Zamboanga Airport and out to Manila.

In a letter to Limoso, my uncle, the President of Taiwan, expressed the undying gratitude of the Taiwanese people. In a way, he expressed my gratitude as well, writing:

Office of the President of Republic of China

Taipei, Taiwan ROC

TO: COL Aldred L. Limoso (Retired)—Regional Director, National Intelligence Coordinating Agency, Region 9

Words cannot begin to express the debt of gratitude that I can express to you for your intrepid bravery, sacrifice, and dedication in the actions that led to the successful return of Republic of China national, Chang An-Wei, a.k.a. Evelyn Chang, back to her homeland. The selfless actions undertaken by yourself and your colleagues are seldom found in the world we find ourselves in today, and it is inspiring to have the opportunity to write and to thank a man such as yourself.

While the details of the operation have been held as classified and close-hold information even from my office, I have been assured that your actions were critical in the support of Chang An-Wei, and I extend my deepest and sincerest message of appreciation for your work. I implore you to continue combating these Abu Sayyaf terrorists with all your formidable capability and might, as their neutralization will only mean brighter days for the Philippines and for the Republic of China as well.

Again, I thank you for your aid and most of all, for your sacrifice.

Best regards,
Ma Ying-Jeou
President, Republic of China

The exploits of the Scout Rangers and NICA operatives that day are still virtually unknown in the Philippines. Their names are not remembered there. But they will be here.

- **Colonel Aldred L. Limoso**—Philippine Army (retired); National Intelligence Coordinating Agency Regional Director, Region 9
- **Colonel Eduardo B. Davalan**—Infantry (General Staff

Course), Philippine Army, Regiment Commander, First Scout Ranger Regiment, Special Operation Command, Philippine Army

- **Lieutenant Colonel Dennis V. Eclarin**—Infantry, Philippine Army
- **Major Manuel Juter Gemao**—Infantry, Philippine Army
- **Technical Sergeant Antonio L. Relao**—Infantry, Philippine Army
- **Staff Sergeant Erwin B. Agustin**—Infantry, Philippine Army
- **Staff Sergeant Zaldimar P. Liban**—Infantry, Philippine Army
- **Sergeant Amilhasbi T. Adil**—Infantry, Philippine Army
- **Corporal Elbryan A. Canedo**—Infantry, Philippine Army
- **Corporal George Vicente Wigan**—Infantry, Philippine Army
- **Corporal Gil G. Ordonio**—Infantry, Philippine Army
- **Corporal Jasper C. Geronimo**— Infantry, Philippine Army
- ███████████████—National Intelligence Coordinating Agency case officer, Region 9
- ███████████████—National Intelligence Coordinating Agency case officer, Region 9

Ranks are dated 2013.

ACKNOWLEDGMENTS

"Books are treasures," my family's motto begins. I'm not so vain as to claim that this book, my halting attempt to share the story of my life and the saga of Evelyn Chang's rescue, might be seen as a treasure by others. But there are treasures in it. They're in the stories that the remarkable people in this book have shared with me and allowed me to share with you.

I cannot express my gratitude or my admiration strongly enough, beginning with Evelyn herself. As I was finishing this book, I learned something about her that I had never known, the depths of her despair during captivity. I would not have had that strength. She remains an inspiration for me, and I am grateful to have been given a chance to let you see her the way I do.

That's true, too, for her devoted sister, Angela, her brother, Richard, and her niece, Jennifer, who all worked tirelessly to win Evelyn's release. Angela in particular showed remarkable courage, poise, and wisdom, never losing sight of her goal while also coping with a ravenous Taiwanese press and the often-byzantine political currents in Taiwan.

I must also acknowledge the family of Eric Hsu, the man whose violent death may have come while protecting Evelyn the night the terrorists kidnapped her. We will never know. However, as I shared privately one evening after meeting Eric's nephew for the first time, I truly believe that his cosmic fate saved lives that night, rousing the entire resort and forcing the terrorists to flee with Evelyn before more blood could be shed.

I'm also indebted to Nick, Aldred, ███████████████, and all the Scout Rangers and NICA operatives, not just for their heroism in the moment but also for their support and encouragement as I searched for the best way to tell their story. Without their insights, without their willingness to share details with me that had been hidden—even from me—at the time, this book might never have been completed. All my personal revenue proceeds from this book will be given to them as donations to causes or purposes of their choice.

I am also deeply grateful for the intrepid Joe Felter for introducing me to the great Dennis Eclarin. I am truly amazed at what they both did for a stranger. They were key links in a steel chain that connects the Long Gray Line everywhere, and Evelyn Chang was freed from her bonds and undoubtedly survived this ordeal thanks to these two good men.

I'm grateful to my uncle for setting an example for our family to follow for all time—it is hard to imagine that anyone in our family will ever match his achievements, or bear the lonely burden of leading an entire country. The quiet dignity and strength he has always demonstrated under extreme duress is something that I will always appreciate and admire.

I could not have written this book had it not been for the help and guidance I received from my mother and my father. As I neared the end of the process, my mother became a sounding board and, occasionally, a fact-checker. She has always encouraged me to push myself harder, and she's also always reined me in when I pushed too hard and too far. She did it again here.

I also want to thank my life partner and wife, Paula, for being the undying support and love that I've needed to reach my full potential—she makes me twice the man I would be without her. I never understood the Chinese word for "peace" (安), the combination of the character for "woman" and "house," until Paula entered mine. I would never have been able to pursue this project and put the time in without her handling every aspect of my life to leave me undistracted to juggle writing this book.

I want to thank my great friends Damon Lau, Deb Lau, Barron Lau, and Juri Maeda for inspiring me to share my story with the world. Sharing an old masonry house together in Marrakesh for a wedding over more than a few drinks led to years of gracious hosting, guidance, and advice from the Lau family. This book would not exist had it not been for their generosity and support.

I also am grateful for my dear friend and mentor, Matt Pecot. He was the first to respond when many shied away, and to this day he continues to support me as the most dependable and reliable business partner one could hope for at Blackpanda.

They say that writing is a solitary pursuit. That's a myth. I've discovered that writing a book is a team sport, and this book had a hell of a team, including my agents, Byrd Leavell and Dan Milaschewski; Selena James, my visionary editor; and Jason Kirk, a gifted wordsmith who worked his magic on my rough prose, showing me how to turn a collection of stories and observations into a book.

I am defined by West Point breaking me down and building me back up, kicking and screaming the entire way, and then waiting for me at the finish line to clap me on the back. I will always be grateful for the hard lessons the academy taught me that my father and mother loved me too much to teach me as a child. It is the greatest educational institution on the planet bar-none and I will forever carry the core values of duty, honor, and country that West Point instilled into me. Go Bandits.

I am also marked for all time by the 1st Special Forces Regiment, or better known as the "Green Berets." This is the greatest organization that I have ever been part of and will be proud to the day I die that I walked among those legends for a brief wrinkle in time. *De Oppresso Liber.*

I'm also grateful to the writer who helped me shape these stories. An older guy, a bit of a dinosaur, a chain-smoking, coffee-swilling throwback to the old days of rewrite men and ink-stained wretches, he taught me a lot as he guided me through the stories of my own life and helped me pick the right words to make those stories come to life. It's amazing what an old man (who insisted on remaining anonymous) can do with a noun, a verb, and a little bit of compassion. During our time together, he shared with me a hard lesson learned over his years, a bit of a secret to life that has resonated with me ever since. When we first met outside a café in the Chelsea district of New York City years ago, he shared a poignant story about his own struggles with his ailing father—forgiveness can set you free from the pain and suffering that we feel every day.

Forgiveness for oneself, for one's family, for one's friends—and most of all, even for one's enemies.

They're treasures. All. And I am in their debt.

ABOUT THE AUTHOR

Photo © Gabriel Aiden Ng

Gene Yu was born in Concord, Massachusetts, in 1979, and entered the United States Military Academy at West Point in 1997, where he majored in computer science and graduated top of his class. Gene served in Korea and Japan as a US Army Armor and Special Forces officer. He deployed for four combat tours in Iraq and the southern Philippines, and is a recipient of two Bronze Star Medals and the Combat Infantryman Badge. In 2015, Gene founded Blackpanda Group, a cybersecurity insurance and emergency response services company headquartered in Singapore, and currently serves as the CEO. Gene is also an alumnus of Johns Hopkins School of Advanced International Studies and Stanford Graduate School of Business.